T0064309

SUDDENLY SINGLE AT SIXTY

A GUIDE TO OVERCOMING THE LOSS OF YOUR SIGNIFICANT OTHER

Patricia J. Koprucki

BALBOA.
PRESS
A DIVISION OF HAY HOUSE

Balboa Press books may be ordered through booksellers or by contacting:

Balboa Press
A Division of Hay House
1663 Liberty Drive
Bloomington, IN 47403
www.balboapress.com.au
1 (877) 407-4847

Because of the dynamic nature of the Internet, any web addresses or links contained in this book may have changed since publication and may no longer be valid. The views expressed in this work are solely those of the author and do not necessarily reflect the views of the publisher, and the publisher hereby disclaims any responsibility for them.

Neither this book nor any of its contents constitute medical, psychological, legal or other professional advice. The author does not dispense medical advice or opinions, nor does the author prescribe the use of any technique as a form of treatment for physical, emotional or medical problems in this book, whether directly or indirectly. The author does not dispense legal counsel or advice or provide legal opinions in this book, whether directly or indirectly. The reader seeking a medical opinion and/or medical advice is encouraged to consult with a physician or other qualified expert. The reader seeking a legal opinion and/or legal advice is encouraged to consult with an attorney. The author's intent is only to offer information of a general nature to help the reader in a quest for emotional and spiritual well-being. In the event the reader uses any of the information in this book for himself or herself, neither the author nor the publisher assumes responsibility for such actions by the reader.

Print information available on the last page.

ISBN: 978-1-5043-1418-3 (sc)
ISBN: 978-1-5043-1419-0 (e)

Balboa Press rev. date: 09/12/2019

Contents

I dedicate this book to my husband, Mark—my joy and inspiration. Thank you for filling our many years together with love and laughter, and for the unwavering support you gave so generously to all of us, including our cat, Boo. Thanks for the trips to Europe, the Caribbean, Carbondale and the South Side of Chicago. (And Leroy, kudos for teaching me to run from a knife and duck from a gun.) RIP, Mark, and may the kind of peace be with you that we had in the Sixties, God bless 'em.

My heartfelt gratitude to:

My husband, Mark, my father, Bill, my mother, Joan and my sister, Elizabeth, for being in my corner.

My great-nephew, Bakouri, whose artwork creates hope and happiness.

My editors, Geoff Smith and my sister, Elizabeth, for their tireless encouragement and insightful guidance.

My high school English teacher, Ms. Margaret Crowe, for setting the bar high.

My mother-in-law, Martha, for being there for me just as her son always was.

My gurus, Hugh Woodall and Cathy Cooper, who continue to inspire me.

My friend and mentor, Betty, for the European adventures and for her laughter, listening and guidance through the years.

My friend and mentor, Carol, a talented author and website designer, and a caring animal rescuer, for making me laugh and keeping it real; may she Rest in Peace.

The lovely dogs who add so much sparkle and joy to our lives: Twix, Piper and Minnie Pearl.

Prologue

"It was not worth feeling what small, fleeting joy life brings ... And so, 'im carve out 'im heart, lock it down in a chest, and hide the chest from the world."

—Tia Dalma,
Pirates of the Caribbean: Dead Man's Chest

Performing cardiovascular surgery on yourself without anesthesia. That sums up the feeling when it's time to make the decision that pales all others. Time to pinch-hit for the one who helped make you who you are, because he is unconscious and wired to the wall. The one who stood by you and laughed with you into the night. The one who finished your sentences. The one who picked you out and lifted you up.

Now it's your turn to hold the remote, and it isn't pretty. Those who call themselves doctors, accompanied by their fawning minions, look at you strangely, with bludgeoning, unwanted sympathy. "First, do no harm." Their patronizing is harm enough. Do not go gentle. Take notes and names. And get an autopsy. But all legalities aside, you'll know when it's time to let him go, to let nature take its course, to disempower the technology and empower your soul mate's dignity. To take him beyond the poking and the prodding, the needles and the questions, beyond your own denial.

Some deaths are harder on the dying than others. A person who dies quickly and unexpectedly would likely rejoice if he were still able, that he never had to go to a nursing home and was never saddled with the "slow-moving, ugly, dependent neediness of old age," as my sister, Elizabeth, puts it. He would be glad that he was never held hostage by confusion and uncontrollable appendages, that he "lived fast, died young, and left a good-looking corpse."[1] Who can envision James Dean as an old man? Let the beautiful memories crystallize, and add new positive memories to your bank, keeping brain plaque at bay! Even if a long nursing home stint preceded death, that stay and the longing for home that accompanied it are now mercifully over.

I once knew an elderly woman whose dog, Happy, died. She immediately got a new dog and named her "Happy" too. Some gaps can never be filled but can morph into new gaps that can. You, chance, and your spiritual guide can work together to fill them. That process of gap filling is an alternative art form to the grieving process, but one that can require just as much creativity. We're all looking for "Happy"—and we deserve him. So get out of the boat and start swimming. Or dog-paddling—as Happy 1 or 2 eagerly would have done!

Your soul mate cannot rescue you now. But if he was anything like my soul mate, he taught you to rescue yourself. He is with you and guiding you. He will be with you at midnight when you're dealing with some arrogant Technoprick trying to "walk you through" a connectivity issue that Technoprick insists is at "your end." (By the way, *always* insist that customer "support" stay on

---

[1] John Derek in the 1949 film *Knock on Any Door*

the phone while you navigate his company's allegedly user-friendly website, which was created not for the customer, but to save the company phone time and paper.) Your soul mate taught you for a reason—to give you the strength for Now.

No one will measure up to your soul mate if you use the same yardstick that you measured him by. So use a different style of yardstick—maybe go Euro/metric or decide height just isn't that important. Or stand Prospect against a doorframe and draw a line to see how tall he is and whether you'll be able to wear heels. Or see how far he can throw a lasso or whether he can drive a stick shift. Or how long he can shut up so you can make your point.

Your life is a relay race—your soul mate took the baton first. That he won't be the final runner does not denigrate the role he played, or your victory, which will also be his. His initial sprint set the tone for things to come—the pace, your expectations, and your own finish line. Your soul mate had the will to take that risk with you, back when you had no track record. The final runner, if he crosses the finish line, will only do so because your soul mate led the charge. They are a team. Although your soul mate would never have passed the baton in his own lifetime, he has more wisdom now. He has seen the final finish line and recognizes that it's defined by connections too intricate to clearly understand from our current vantage point.

Since you are reading this book you have recognized that you can't hide in a hole or in a virtual world of electric shadows (and not for want of trying). These escapes, while temporarily satisfying and necessary, will not bring nirvana.

You are ready to sparkle, maybe with cheap jewelry and clothes from the Junior Department but shine you will. You have grieved long enough. You'll never feel or look as good as you do today. NOW IS THE TIME to get out of the comfort zone that has protected you from the most dangerous hazards. You've survived the darkness, now you must emerge from it.

I

When "We" Becomes "I"—Death, Divorce and Disaster

My life changed drastically when I lost my husband of more than twenty-nine years, my sole companion and soul mate. In addition to encouraging me on every personal level—exercise, appearance, health—he also mentored my business and personal life, until the day before he went on life support.

There is no room for denial during that final conversation. Existence is reduced to an oozing wound. The tightly knit cliques of newly minted medical residents were no match for the raging infection.

Divorcees and primary caretakers also know this pain. When I represented clients in divorce proceedings, I observed firsthand the pain inflicted by separation. The hardest to watch were custody battles—the newfound uncomfortable poverty, the smothering by family members trying but failing to help. The loss of loved ones to debilitating disease can also trigger grief—the brutal, slow-moving tsunami of progressing Alzheimer's erasing its host, aggressive tumors ravaging multiple organs via stealth attacks.

1

When disaster strikes, do what you must do to get by. Airline passengers are advised to put on their own oxygen masks before assisting others, even their children. Define your oxygen. What lets you breathe? Find your peaceful place, even if at first, it's only in dreams or on the edge of consciousness.

II

Surviving the Holidays and Other Milestones

Raw survival is the first stepping-stone toward your reentry into the dating world. And one of the biggest initial challenges is coping with the painful memories and feelings of loneliness that the holidays can provoke.

Even if you and your soul mate didn't make a huge production out of holidays, surviving that first set may well zap most of your emotional energy. But the great thing about the holidays is that you know they are coming and can plan accordingly.

Giving yourself time and space to mourn is particularly important during holidays and other occasions you celebrated together. You may not be able fully to prepare for the feelings you will experience, so expect the unexpected and brace yourself for occasional feelings of unpreparedness. Pushing yourself toward exhaustion by pursuing a frantic schedule—the proverbial "keeping busy"—may not be the answer. Hospice or other agencies may offer a calm in the Christmas storm—special programs that help survivors through difficult times, where you will not be labeled or judged. Participating in one of these programs may help you share your losses and triumphs with fellow survivors in unthreatening surroundings.

These programs may also increase your arsenal of tools for coping with the holidays and give you the chance to help others and thus connect with the universe. You have probably already developed coping techniques that could be immensely helpful to others. The process of sharing what you've learned will give both you and your fellow survivors much to be thankful for at Thanksgiving. And at Christmas, Hanukah, or Eid, your generosity will bestow a gift far more lasting and valuable than any Black Friday special.

If you have already experienced your first Thanksgiving and Christmas without your soul mate, pat yourself on the back—that's a big deal. Take a moment or two to note a couple of things that helped you get through your days since his death—techniques that you'd feel comfortable sharing with others who might be inspired to develop their own holiday coping mechanisms. Activities might include spending time with your children, parents, siblings or your dog if you are lucky enough to still have them. Or watching something hilarious on TV. Not laughing at the preposterous requires way more energy than you'll want to expend right now. Visualize yourself walking along a beach with your favorite five-year-old grandchild as he looks up at you with trusting, joy-filled eyes.

Briefly noting some of the things that have worked for you will prepare you to help others in need:

1._____

_____

2._____

_____

Now is the time to establish new traditions. If you feel like being totally alone for a particular holiday, your mind may be telling you that that's what you need. Trying to "snap out of it" may be the worst thing you can do. Sometimes a totally quiet day away from the challenges of paperwork, moving, changing jobs, or other transitions that seem to drag on forever can be a welcome change and opportunity for reflection. If you are concerned that a quiet day partially devoted to acknowledging your sadness might drag you into a depression, consider seeking input about this from a counselor. You'll know soon enough whether this works for you—a day or two when you allow yourself to be sad but also to give thanks for the years that you and your soul mate shared.

A. Travel

Where you spend your transitional holidays can be crucial as you gradually fill the gaping void. I was very lucky indeed when my brother-in-law, Bakr, kindly treated our family with a trip to South Beach on that first holiday. My then-teenage nephew and my sister helped me more during those days than I could ever describe—we laughed hard, ate lobster, and drank Starbucks on the beach under blue-and-white striped umbrellas. The calm and laughter stilled the sadness for a while.

Most any trip can provide fun and peace of mind— where you go is much less important than who your travel companions are. I personally don't enjoy trips with large groups of women—they sometimes count their tips too meticulously, occasionally even using those annoying credit card–sized tip calculators fished out of ridiculously large totes. Their chatter and gossip that can grate on my last nerve, particularly during the holidays. Even if the conversations were loftier, it would still be too noisy—too much yick yack on any intellectual level disrupts karma—when they're talking, you don't get to.

You probably have a select few trustworthy and comfortable friends, but keep the trip short unless you have traveled with them before and know you can tolerate them for something longer. Flying is a little more challenging now due to your age and to the lines and the rules that affect packing, so you might want to travel with someone at least your first time out of the gate. If you have mobility problems, or if you're just not sure that you can walk those airport distances, don't hesitate to order a wheelchair. If you take a carry-on, by all means make it a spinner—they're much easier to manipulate than the old-school wheeled case, and easier on your body than the shoulder-strap carry-ons we used to drag around before the wheel(ed suitcase) was invented. If you haven't bought a great smartphone yet, I highly recommend the iPhone—it's *very* easy to use, doing what it's supposed to do and what it logically should do. You'll have to play around on it a bit, do some trial and error—a perfect vacation pastime at an airport, in the back seat of a taxi, or on a balcony or beach. View technology as your new playground.

Speaking of airports, here is a fun game to play as you people-watch. Get a front row seat wherever there is people traffic. Tell whomever you're traveling with that the fifth person who walks by will be your travel companion's future spouse. You can create all kinds of sub-rules, like which direction they have to be walking in, how to count a group that all walk by at the same time, gender restrictions, etc. It will make you smile, and that will make you much more approachable than if you were hunched over your phone. Airports and airplanes are rife with potential for both business and pleasure. Carry your business cards and dress like you mean it. Only you can define and complete your mission.

You don't miss someone as much if you're not tethered to your usual holiday routine that you shared with him. Watching the beautiful people helps you figure out how to enhance your own beauty and inspires you to become more glamorous. There are many singles enjoying the holiday in South Beach and other vacation destinations, so you don't feel boxed into a world filled with happy families around Christmas trees. You might want to save Disney World and other family-oriented hotspots for a later trip. Why torture yourself now? There will be time for those sorts of holidays when you are farther along in the process and you can enjoy them with children.

B. Gifts

Select a small gift that symbolizes a quality of your soul mate that you loved and respected and put it into a gift bag along with a poem or short narrative about him. Give one to each family member, and one to yourself. If he loved to barbeque, you might select a bottle of his favorite sauce and write a short note about a 4th of July barbecue that he threw. If he was a dog lover, buy a small replica of his favorite dog and write about loyalty, compassion, and forgiveness. These gifts keep his memory alive in others' hearts as well as your own.

If his mother is still with you, count your blessings. Find a tiny picture of him, place it in a locket, and send it to her. It will reassure her that you will always remember and honor his memory even if she already knew that you would. Only you and she can fully share the bond to him. We're all afraid of not being remembered, so remember him and his mother generously, and with kindness, humor, and respect.

Some companies sell tasteful and reasonably priced Christmas ornaments that can be personalized to bear your loved one's birth and death dates or other information. Or you might design your own ornaments to reflect an interest of your soul mate or one of his many victories.

Buy yourself a gift too. Get it on sale after Christmas. Do it to celebrate surviving December 25. Make it something you think that he might have picked out for you. Who's to say he's not influencing your choice of gifts even now? You will hear his voice often, sometimes when you least expect it, although he speaks differently now—not always in words but in images, echoes. His message will usually console you although sometimes he just tells you to get off your ass. He will come to you in dreams, and although you might expect these dreams to disturb you upon awakening, they rarely if ever have that effect. Usually there is a comforting message if you clear away the roadblocks of logic and reason and observe the imagery that distils the message to its core.

Anniversaries can be bitches—probably harder than all the rest—the day you met, got engaged, your wedding date. As with other holidays, plan ahead. Buy yourself a white cake with icing and enjoy it with expensive ice cream and lime-flavored Perrier, which tastes as close to a gin and tonic as you can get without alcohol. Don't do the cake and ice cream thing too often or you'll lose the slim figure you've been struggling to maintain, but don't deprive yourself of everything all the time either.

Art projects are great for holidays, birthdays, and anniversaries. Make a diorama with skeleton dolls bought in an after-Halloween sale and call it "'Til Death Do Us Part." This ironic creation announces that even death can't part you. Dress like a zombie bride at Halloween. He would have loved that, even if he would never have gone as your zombie groom. Peruse the kitchen utensil section of Wal-Mart and various hardware aisles at Home Depot. Art projects will jump out at you. Mobiles made from pie pans. Volcanoes that spew liquid glitter lava. Creativity may find artistic form as you grieve, particularly during the emotional chaos of the holidays. Now is the time to get in touch with your inner Dali, who will greet you with a wink and a smile. This is much more likely to happen when drinking coffee infused with whipped cream (Caveat: The "no fat" version does not cut it!)

Your own birthday may be easy compared to his birthday, or it may be just the opposite. It all depends on how you celebrated these events. Hopefully you have saved some birthday gifts and cards from your soul mate. If you decide to give them away, give them to family members who knew and treasured him, or to those relatives who would have treasured him the most if they had ever met him. Your soul mate's birthday can sometimes cause you to pause and reflect upon important moments since his death, things he will never know or be part of—births, deaths, marriages, and other milestones, new pets acquired and loved, even technological developments. Appreciate these things and know that your soul mate is glad that you are now experiencing them for both of you.

Valentine's Day is a great day to regress. Send valentines to your family and sign them with love from you and your dog. Give your grandchildren valentines to send to others. Or give them construction paper, doilies, markers, and stickers and help them make their own, old school. Then ask them to show you how to make an e-valentine with their latest smartphone app. Decorate a shoebox with paper designs to hold all of the valentines your soul mate gave you. Go to a confectioner and buy yourself a fancy satin and lace-topped heart filled with chocolates. Or cupcakes with mile-high icing graced by red plastic hearts. Or a hot pink rhinestone-embellished contact case by Juicy Couture. God knows you deserve it.

My first Valentine's Day I received a beautiful bouquet from my cousin, Heather. It's amazing how people who are a generation younger can understand so fully even though they have never endured what you've been through. Insights by those with clean slates can be remarkable, possibly because they see things freshly and with the hope and innocent wisdom of youth. If you don't have a cousin like that, then be that person for someone else. Remember your friends and family on Valentine's Day, regardless of whether they are alone. Make a note of your friends' and relatives' significant milestones and connect with them on those dates. Comfort can be most comforting when it's least expected.

On a wedding anniversary many years after my soul mate's death my niece and nephew, Ahmed and Rana, surprised me with a lovely music box engraved with our names and our anniversary date. As if that weren't more than enough, they also brought me a small cake and flowers. I hope that you are blessed with treasured relatives like this—and whether or not you are, be that loved one for someone in your family. Go that extra mile.

C. Paying Your Respects

Holidays, anniversaries, and birthdays may find you at the cemetery. You will know when you need to go to his gravesite or touch the urn carrying his ashes. It won't be every day, and you may not need to linger long or even get out of the car. But that physical proximity can be surprisingly comforting and can infuse you with insights as you face a decision, or with strength when you need it most. Releasing balloons with your family at your soul mate's grave on his birthday can be comforting. Delight when thoughtful nieces and nephews leave small toys intertwined with graveside flowers—something to show they were there, that they remember him or wish they had known him, and that life goes on. Collect as many of these empowering moments as possible.

D. Alcohol and Other Pitfalls

Alcohol is often part of holiday festivities. Although it may feel like it's providing at least a temporary panacea, the mo(u)rning after always comes and often with painful consequences. Because you are alone and have to do all of your own grocery shopping and other errands, in addition to your job or retirement activities—and because you are older now—you just don't have time to waste a day in bed with a hangover. Sobriety gives you the best chance of waking up bright and cheerful. Of course, there may be days when you have to force yourself to get out of bed even if you don't have a hangover, but why give yourself another reason to lose a day or a half day? You need your beauty sleep and the energy to get things done, even if it's just binge-watching on Netflix. You have an agenda.

If you know you have an alcohol problem, or if someone has told you that you do even if you don't agree, find a good counselor for an objective opinion on the issue and follow his or her instructions. This will likely include going to AA where you will find support among your peers and help when you need it, and where you may learn to recognize a Higher Power that will help you with your addiction as well as with your grieving process.[2] Holidays are often particularly challenging for alcoholics who celebrate the season at bars where Christmas tchotchkes adorn the mirrors and walls and holiday cheer flows free and easy. Remember, you're driving yourself now. And even if you're not, do you really want to entrust your keys and your life to someone who, although sober, may have a bad traffic record or be distracted by his or her own holiday turmoils?

Each year the holidays, birthdays, and anniversaries roll around again—some years are easy, some difficult. Each year on his birthday you will probably count how many years he has been gone and how old he would have been. On your wedding anniversary you will calculate how many years you would have been married. Your relationship with your soul mate never really ends, so if you do find a new significant other, don't apologize for maintaining your prior connection on certain special days (and understand that he may also have important, unseverable bonds that he similarly treasures and honors). Although you only committed "'til death do us part,"

---

[2] If you have a drinking problem but don't think that permanent abstinence is the right solution for you, you might consider a program such as Moderation Management, which, in its own words, seeks to help people "accept personal responsibility for choosing and maintaining their own path, whether moderation or abstinence." https://www.moderation.org/about_mm/whatismm.html.

There are also thousands of outpatient rehabilitation centers that use completely secular, evidence-based approaches as opposed to AA's 12-step program. Call a clinic near you and ask them about their methods. Consult with your doctor and with substance abuse professionals who may help you decide which program is right for you.

you will never be able fully to divide him from you, so stop trying and let it flow. It is what it is. Be glad that it was. There is no such thing as absolute closure.

Cut yourself some slack at the holidays and other special occasions. It's okay to say no to friends' invitations if it would just be too awkward. It's also okay for you to invite guests if that's what feels right. Everything might feel a little awkward right at first, but it's up to you to acknowledge, accept and eventually overcome that awkwardness. If you accept an invitation, take your own car so you can escape if the walls start closing in or the tears start to flow. So, what if you're at a wedding that costs $175 a plate and you leave before dinner? Congratulate yourself for having shown up at all. Many who were freely imbibing may not remember your abrupt departure, or even that you were there at all. Those who matter will remember, and they will understand.

III

Packaging Your Product: Putting the Best You Out There

A. Hair and Makeup

Now that you're ready to get back out there, your most important trio is Hair, Makeup, and Weight. Bottom line: try not to look like a fat Dutch boy in man shoes. My nephew, Mohammed, said the haunted house in Oldtown, Florida, was "scawey." Haunted houses are supposed to be scary. You should not be.

Short hair can only be worn by certain women—Rooney Mara, for example. Obtain professional advice on the short vs. long issue and assess that advice carefully. Refuse to be pigeonholed into short hair just because you are no longer twenty. If you have a small head, sharp, defined features, and doe eyes to die for, or if you receive compliments after downsizing your lock length, you might seriously consider working a "Twiggy" do for a while. But change it up now and then.

Pay up. Don't self-dye any more than you would self-medicate. If you can't afford ongoing professional hair maintenance, go in for the works at least once and get a thorough consultation about which affordable products best flatter you. Investing in a great stylist whom you tip well will not only improve your appearance and therefore your outlook but will also net you a great listener and friend. Don't choose someone who's always in a big fat hurry. Any stylist can improve your appearance the first shot she gets at you, if you go in looking scraggly enough (and you will). But how does she do on the second or third crack, when you're getting your style on and your confidence back (and you will)? One side shorter than the other, and not by design? Don't let it slide.

Some salons invite the telling of one's life story. There will be days during this challenge-filled time when silence is golden, so consider whether you want a chatty environment when you choose a permanent stylist. Sometimes you just want to listen to Chinese water music. The hairdressing experience must generate epiphany, hope and renewal. Soiled towels and mindless chatter interfere with the Process of You. So, speak up or move on. Refuse to be rushed.

Presenting your stylist with a photo of what you want to look like can be very entertaining. (I personally enjoy the stylist's reaction when I say I want to look like Charlize Theron.) This is also a good way to see whether your relationship will work—does she get real with you without taking that patronizing tone assumed only by the painfully beautiful with flawless smiles? Does she helpfully suggest how another of your great features might be better emphasized by an alternate do?

As for color, make it natural—think caramel highlights. Not too platinum or silver blond, as these shades can be mistaken for gray. If you color, maintain it ruthlessly. Schedule dye jobs well in advance. The hair appointment, like the periodic colonoscopy, is non-negotiable.

Regarding makeup, don't bother getting a makeover at a department store unless you want to spend an entire paycheck on a tiny compact. These overly made-up women hawking their wares will exploit you. Because they are seated closely to you in a canned environment of false intimacy, they will feel free to brutally insult you. Don't give them that power. You are a well-trained street fighter; your skills having been sharpened by your years and by your relentless interrogation of doctors throughout your soul mate's illness. It wouldn't be a fair fight. You have more important battles to win right now, no time for toothy, cheerful suggestions. And what's up with the white coats? Are they chemists?

Go online to research which makeup is the best—and order it. Indecision is your enemy. Don't waste time driving to remote malls and subjecting yourself to the young and beautifuls' attempts to demean you. Know your strengths, and the value of your time.

B. Clothes

We all have that favorite turquoise dress. Or if turquoise doesn't do it for you, pick the color that rocks your psyche. And let it be *real* color, no drab colonial blue or moss green. And no ridiculous yuppie colors like screaming hot pink or electric lime green, except for accent colors or accessories.

Pay up. Cheap leopard spandex tights are out, but animal prints can kick up your style if used sparingly. And instead of adding charm to your look, grosgrain ribbon will age you. (TradeUp, whom you will meet later in this book, adores grosgrain. He is the sorry exception to the otherwise predictable rule.) The particular color or fabric in the abstract is not important, however. What matters most is how an ensemble or an accessory makes you feel.

The Great Clothing Dilemma is black vs. color. Black is slimming. Color, not so much. But beware the myths, i.e., that horizontal stripes make you look fat. If you find a properly ruched top, horizontal-type folds, if curved, can be very slimming—and in bright colors too. Resolve this dilemma by wearing what makes you feel powerful, unstoppable and kick-ass.

Coats are problematic because they add girth. The more flattering the coat, the less warmth it provides. If you have a Vicuna coat, don't give it away without an appraisal. Especially a coat that has a Saks Fifth Avenue label, like a coat that used to belong to my great-grandmother. One Vicuna sweater may be worth five grand or more. But don't wear it either, because it will make you look dowdy, particularly if it has no real shape, Vicuna though it may be. Don't wear it, but don't throw it away either. We just can't pull that trigger.

Jeans that fit can take you to the stars. No one likes to try on jeans. It's boring. All that denim, and all jeans looking so alike on the rack or the shelf. But take whatever time it takes to get that perfect pair. Then buy two of them.

If you're not careful, your closet can become a museum of Days Gone By. Each garment holds a memory—perfect moments, youthful fantasies. Maybe you have a lucky suit. Or maybe you're afraid to throw away the clothes you wore to your husband's funeral, afraid to lose that connection, afraid of not honoring his memory. And yet, you avoid looking at it. GO NOW, THIS VERY MOMENT, TO YOUR CLOSET AND THROW AWAY SOMETHING THAT DOESN'T MAKE YOU CRAZY HAPPY. Start with one thing only. Then if you get going, you might decide to continue the process. Pitch what fails to flatter. If you can't bear to part with it, consign it to a trash bag and store it out of sight. Some distance from your dowdy oldies will create perspective. Maybe you'll garner the strength to donate them in a couple of weeks. And if you do, get a receipt.

C. Weight and Height

Get out, get in motion, and take it off. Some programs work very well, particularly those requiring in-person meetings. You get to eat a lot of fruit, and the meetings are wonderful social events. The leader makes jokes and although most attendees are seriously committed to losing weight, the approach is filled with humor, kindness, and camaraderie. Go just for the fun of it.

Gyms have germs, and some of them walk on two legs. Men in midlife, for instance. Then there are the lipstick housewives who have never and will never work, prancing around in brand-name workout clothing they wouldn't have dreamed of buying on sale. For them it's about feeding vanity, not about maintaining health. They will not acknowledge you—they keep to their cliques, just like they did in high school. Forget them. Grab your sani-wipes, put on your armor, and go for broke.

Walk the dog. Gradually increase the length of the walk. A dog will tell you a lot if you listen. On calm mornings he will take you to new places, geographically and spiritually. Follow your dog's lead and surrender to these moments.

D. Shoes

A small heel helps us all. And for God's sake, get yourself some boots. Check out the suede if you must, but when the band plays that final song, it's leather that will take you home. Do NOT worry about durability. We want to look good *today*.

Boots have The Power. The power to change your gait, your demeanor and possibly your life. You may scare people as you click along challenging the power dynamics in whatever forum you practice your trade or play your games. But ass-kicking, sidewalk-clicking boots will earn you the respect you deserve. Naming them increases their power: "The Enforcers" has a take charge ring to it.

Wearing boots is much like drinking a real Coke. Real women don't wear boat like, soft-soled flats, nor do they drink Diet Cokes. And real men don't drink them either. They don't pour saccharine into their highly metabolized systems. But make no mistake. These very same real men *want* to be intimidated by the power and confidence of a svelte you in boots. So, strap 'em up, ladies, keep the line moving, and leave that cowboy in the dust if you want to win his heart.

Neurologists may have a hard time explaining why acupuncture works, but it sometimes does. Men can't explain why boots bring them to their knees, but they do. So, wear them well, but not too often, lest they lose their power.

If you decide to date a short man, wear the boots anyway, and if he shuts his yapper about it then you might want to reconsider any "no shorties" policy that you might have. A man who's willing to keep his trap shut about the things he doesn't like may be THE ONE. Only a real man can love a woman who is taller than he. You're not necessarily looking to avoid all short men, just judgmental short men who talk too much and try to give you to-do lists.

The most powerful shoe is the "Problem Solver." You may see these shoes, which are usually red, in the shop windows at Christmastime. Or perhaps a barely mauve snakeskin spike heel. Deep down you know these shoes will be life-changing. Trust these moments of inspiration but learn to distinguish them from shopaholism. Problem Solvers are usually round-toed with a bit of a platform. Collect as many Problem Solvers as you have problems. You cannot shop for these shoes—they must find you. And they will.

Shopping for shoes or clothing on the internet can be deceptively time consuming and costly, considering the shipping costs and the time it takes to box something up and return it if it doesn't do you justice. It's difficult to gauge whether a particular size or color will flatter, and whether it will arrive on time for an upcoming event. And it's more important now than ever for you to get up and away from the computer and into the real world of store clerks, friends, acquaintances and any prospects you may encounter while shopping. These interactions can be confidence builders and provide you with a needed change of venue. And you can peruse various clothing departments—the junior department for example—to assess the latest trends and get a sense of the big fashion picture. It's so much better than scrolling through hundreds of small pictures of various tunic sweaters as you wonder whether they will fit and flatter.

E. Halloween

When in disguise you assume no risk of rejection. Zombie Cinderella may be a little honked off when the man she met at a Halloween party takes Zombie Dorothy home instead. But on the upside, he still doesn't know Cinderella's name. And by the way, she couldn't tell whether he was going as Santa Claus or forgot to wear a costume.

Halloween is one of the few nights when staying at home is a man-meeting option. Whether it's Dad or Mom taking them around may depend, in the context of divorced couples who share parenting time, upon which day your village lets the rug rats out to pillage and burn. Be kind to the children. This will endear you to them even if you do have a two-inch mole hanging off of your nose that isn't part of your costume.[3] At least for today, you'll fit in. And don't be stingy with the candy. You don't want that temptation around tomorrow, particularly if Halloween's promises go unfulfilled.

Career-oriented costumes are always fun—a nurse or policewoman or pirate. Whatever regalia you choose, let it reflect the Best Version of You. Career-themed costumes tell the observer that your future doesn't consist of staring at the TV all day and eating bonbons. Send that message from the start. You want him to know right away that you're not inclined to be at his beck and call.

Costume accessories can also come in handy. As a policewoman you'll have the tools close at hand to fend off the unsuspecting bad apples who come to your front door. That Lockdown Look never fails to intimidate. Just as effective is a first responder–themed costume: firewoman, military mama, fighter pilot or action heroine. Teach important lessons there in your front hall: "Expect the unexpected," and/or, "It's All About Me."

Avoid costumes that are frightening such as dragons, dinosaurs or other wildlife with terrifying teeth. Remember, you are dealing with children. Also avoid any costumes involving electricity. Flashing lights are too big of a safety hazard and could necessitate calling real rescuers whose own costumes would detract from your own.

Wear short skirts if you dare, but please go with black tights to hide the varicose veins and cellulite. A long shawl can

---

[3] And speaking of cosmetic idiosyncrasies, buy a good mirror (at least 10X magnification) and hang it near your door so you can catch any mascara smudges or stray bits of spinach embellishing your teeth. You need to catch these flaws yourself now that you're on your own.

be draped mysteriously over these outfits for a vampire aura. Value what you have but show it judiciously.

F. Health

Listen to your body. Exercise has multiple benefits if done regularly and not in random bursts. Even if you have always been an athlete, you may be more fragile now than you look or want to acknowledge. Seek advice from competent, trained experts before you embark upon an exercise regimen. Your own body will often tell you if you have done too much, but sometimes it waits a day or two to let you know, which can be confusing. If you begin exercising after not working out for a long period of time, beware. And if you suffer a setback, then go through physical therapy and are pain free, don't jump right back into your old ways too soon (or in some cases at all) because you think you are "cured." It may take awhile for the body to restrengthen, even if you are no longer experiencing the pain associated with the condition.

Dealing with doctors who marginalize the elderly is a potential problem, but not if you take an active role in managing your healthcare. Doctors' appointments and hospitalizations can be more difficult now that your soul mate is no longer serving as your advocate. So, find a new advocate—perhaps a family member or similarly situated friend. Take charge of your medical destiny.

Several ways in which you might begin advocating for yourself are:

1.) Prepare a list of your questions and fax or email them to your doctor's office the day before your appointment. Although many offices no longer communicate via fax as frequently as they once did, with faxing you will have a transmittal sheet if you set your machine accordingly. Medical office personnel know that you can prove receipt. Your questions might relate to the doctor's opinion as to causation, diagnosis and prognosis, and your fax could include a history of your current problem and any known medical conditions along with your current medications and drug/food allergies for reference. If you don't get around to sending this list to your physician ahead of time, take it to the appointment with you. If your list is reasonable in length and scope, it can still provide a helpful agenda. Doctors are scientists and therefore likely to appreciate direct, concise questions that save consultation time. A list could also help reduce any stress you may have about possibly forgetting to ask certain questions and will show the doctor that you're a proactive member of your own medical team. Don't leave without a diagnosis or at least a working one if possible, and a clear understanding of any medication or other treatment regimen the doctor recommends.

2.) Many doctors are under enormous pressure to treat a high volume of patients in a short time. This is your life. Speak respectfully but firmly to the occasional "departing doctor" who talks fast and dismisses your concerns as he attempts to exit the consultation room. And beware of doctors too quick to chalk up a condition to "age." Inquire further: "How exactly is the aging process contributing to my condition?" Don't accept a doctor's response as gospel; continue asking any questions you have about his or her response(s). This requires you to listen actively, not just check the questions off your list. If the room is too warm, or if you're uncomfortable in the chair or on

23

the cot, speak up. This puts you in charge. It's up to you to slow down the tempo and get the answers you need and deserve. Keep paper and pen close by so you can take notes. Ask the doctor, PA or nurse to write down the name of the diagnosis if you're not able to or don't trust your memory. When you're in the exam room, keep your paper and pen—or if you're allowed to use it in the exam room, your smartphone—nearby so you can take notes.

3.) Dress appropriately for your medical appointment— like you mean business. This shows respect for the medical profession and more importantly, for yourself. This is not the time for rhinestone-embellished sandals, black toenail polish or nose studs.

4.) Keep an updated list on your computer and/or phone of your medications and dosages, drug and food allergies, medical conditions, and dates and names of significant tests such as a colonoscopy, mammography, bone density and any other lab work. Take this list along with a copy of your healthcare power of attorney to all hospital visits and other medical appointments, unless an emergency doesn't give you the time to collect this information. (Saving the list to your smartphone could prevent that scenario.) Be sure that the agent under your health care power of attorney has an updated copy of this information as well.

5.) Maintain a running log of your medical care, including the date, provider name, and substance of each appointment, test, surgery and hospitalization. Update this immediately after an appointment or phone call.

6.) If uncertain, get a second opinion unless your doctor reasonably believes that obtaining a second opinion might somehow endanger or delay your recovery process. If your life or a major health concern—e.g., your future mobility—is on the line, and if you can do so safely and quickly enough that you are not jeopardizing your medical future, getting a second opinion may provide very valuable information and insight.

7.) Look into the doctor's eyes. Does the surgeon avert his eyes when talking to you after your procedure? This tell is as important sometimes as his words. Warn your new advocate about this as well, since he or she will likely be the one whom your surgeon briefs.

8.) Get a copy of the operating room report. You may not understand it all, but at least you'll have a record of when the surgery was done, the type of anesthesia used, and some understanding of what was done. Many medical records departments open early in the day, so you might try going then. But many are so busy that you might have to follow up on your initial request. Be polite, but as persistent as necessary. You also might be able to access some of your medical records online. Your follow-up must be rigorous and unrelenting.

9.) Choose physicians with outstanding reputations and skills who practice near your home and demonstrate care for their patients. Depending upon your geographical area, you may not have many options and/or you may not be able to schedule an immediate appointment. Accessibility can be extremely important since many times it is not apparent whether medical issues are time-sensitive.

10.) Be assertive when scheduling appointments. If you have developed a good relationship with the scheduler, and if you don't constantly demand special treatment for no reason, your request will usually be taken seriously and granted if humanly possible. Convey flexibility. If the doctor has more than one office, offer to go to the office that's less convenient for you if you're able to make the trip. If you expect to have many questions, ask for an appointment at the end of the day so there isn't a waiting room full of people the doctor needs to see after your appointment. And let the scheduler know why you want that last appointment. This may mean that by the time the doctor sees you, his or her schedule is backed up, but the wait will likely be worth it. When scheduling a medical appointment, write out a very brief outline of the points you want to make. Keep it factual and date-oriented. Help the gatekeeper prepare for you. Impart your deep concern about a medical problem, but only if your concern is genuine. Your tone of voice must reflect your commitment to getting in as soon as possible. Don't whine, snipe, bully, or exaggerate the problem. But tell the scheduler all the facts that help define the urgency of your situation. The scheduler, after consultation with the doctor or nurse in appropriate cases, then has full information as to the degree of urgency. With your soul mate gone, the decision is yours, but sometimes you need some help with it. If you are in doubt, err on the side of going to the ER. Also know that some medical office personnel are willing to schedule specialist appointments for you.

IV

Where the Real Men At? (Not at Spelling Bees)

Real men were never spelling bee champions. Most future real men gravitated toward hunting, fishing, or competitive sports such as football or boxing. You do not want a man who is obsessed with meaningless details. In fact, you want a man who doesn't have time for spelling—and you don't have time, either, now that you're doing everything for yourself. Use spell check if you must, but don't expect men to.

Surprisingly, this obliviousness to detail doesn't apply when they are sizing up the WOTD (woman of their dreams). Their detailed summaries of "what I am looking for" reflect a surprising obsession with perfection and detail, down to the sought-after measurements. If slovenly Santa Claus lookalikes tended to their own beards with the same fervor they use when describing their non-negotiables in mate selection, the world would be a much tidier place.

The real men you are seeking are not lying on the sofa watching TV, nor should you be. No matter how many hours you spend in your own private little Lazy-Girl, you won't meet men there. The electric shadows will not hold your hand in the dark. They won't take you to the emergency room or hassle the doctors on your behalf when you need an advocate.

A real man does not invade your space in the dessert section of an upscale buffet, drumming up a dangling conversation about pecan pie. Conversations about pie are too intimate for an initial encounter. In fact, steer clear of men who dilly-dally around any course at pretentious buffets. Earth to men: buffets are tacky. Men who seek buffets are either grossly overweight or have the attention spans of fruit flies. A real man who wants pie buys one, eats half of it at one sitting and has the active lifestyle to metabolize it.

Real men are not at women's basketball games—unless of course, it is to cheer their daughters or girlfriends on. But the odds are still not in your favor—go to men's games instead. It's all about the numbers.

Some real men patronize the gym. But it's an awkward way to meet them—there in your flattering exercise clothes while someone you know professionally is leering at you through the glass pane in the door as you do your windmills or whatever Latin dance is de rigueur. Like the man in green at the tiny window on the door to Oz, tell him to "come back tomorrow." It's a brutal venue but going there will make you feel so good that it may be worth a few odd ogles.

Real men are not on the golf course. Golf is not a sport, it's a hobby and/or pastime for those athlete wannabes who couldn't make it in true athletic forums. Their only plus is that they'll be out of the house and not bugging you for at least part of every spring and summer weekend. The bad news is they won't be able to serve you on those days, so you'll need to learn how to wield a hammer and an electric drill on your own. Quit sitting around and expecting to be waited on. Enjoy your solitude and the chainsaw's power.

Real men are also at football games. Novocained by the thrill of battle, they are unaware they're freezing their balls off. These men are hazards only if they expect you to sit through that crap with them. If you don't enjoy or at least understand football, let them go on their own.

Real men do not linger for years on dating sites. Anyone camped out there for more than three weeks needs to be avoided. And speaking of dating sites, real men, regardless of how long they may have been "active" on these sites, do not "window peep"—i.e., ask for photographs of you while refusing to provide their own. A real man does not post a lonely picture of himself standing behind a recently thawed supermarket birthday cake, a lone budget store balloon tied loosely to the chair next to him. You do not have time for neediness.

Real men do not hide behind power ties or costumes inherent to their professions. Functionality in professional and casual wear increases the wearer's credibility. Cowboy boots can only be worn by true cowboys who incorporate them into their daily manly routines. Real men don't try to showcase their multitasking abilities by yammering on multiple electronic devices. They are at grocery stores plowing through aisles. People get out of their way because these men command respect and know the value of time. They know what they like, and it isn't fruit—it's ding dongs, by God, and barbeque potato chips (fried, not baked). So, waste no time in the produce department where clear-skinned, overly toned men fondle every last grapefruit.

Real men are in electronics stores. They can install both hardware and software. And they never read manuals, manuals being for sissies. A real man knows where to put plugs, wires and batteries. He knows how to make stuff work.

If you plan to continue your quest for Mr. Right at a big box electronics store, choose your aisles carefully. A real man buys the very best computer he can afford, and it usually works pretty well. Find someone who walks with a swagger and a smile and doesn't give a rat's ass about the computer's online gaming rating. He knows it will work because he knows where to put the plug. He knows you get what you pay for. Real men pay up.

Real men like simple things such as solid colors, guns, and ammo. Things that are what they are and do what they do.

V

Discover What You're Looking for and Don't Start What You Don't Need

A. Defining Your Type

Before beginning your search, know your type. Not unlike the three target universities chosen by college applicants, there are three basic target genres: TradeDown, Jungleboy, and TradeUp. TradeDown is a shoe-in but not so great for your resume. Jungleboy is that big-ass state school up the interstate, a conglomerate of Chicago and the World at Large. TradeUp is that Ivy League school you always knew was a long shot. Either you settle, or you get real in the Jungle. You could aim to strike it big, but now you're wise enough to spot TradeUp's deficiencies, and his lack of authenticity. You see now that ivy may hide decay and sadistic obsession.

1. TradeDown

TradeDown worships you. That creepy guy in high school who feels he has finally made something of himself and makes a decent salary as he counts the days to retirement. Even if

TradeDown is married, he will be delighted to hear from you. If you select him TradeDown will treasure you like no other.

Why? Because *he thinks he's getting a deal.* TradeDown usually has a decent, tenured job in which he does very little, thus freeing himself up to think about you and what might have been. This breed is not known for risk-taking. TradeDown is hard to dislike because he tries so hard. And yet, you find a way.

TradeDown is fundamentally boring—wall clawing, eye-bugging boring. But if you want predictability, and to feel like you matter to someone, then TradeDown is your man.

2. Jungleboy

Jungleboy is a real man with street smarts. His wealth, if he has it, was earned not inherited. He doesn't ride cycles. He's a true athlete. He pumps iron without checking himself out in the mirror. And he doesn't go to tanning booths or take steroids. You will not find him on the golf course. Jungleboy loves boxing, football, basketball, and hard-ass Korean fu jitsu–type sports that require fast movement. Jungleboy is a participant, not a spectator. He knows how to run from a knife and duck from a gun. He is logical and street smart. He's not afraid of up close and personal. He is at home in the vortex of conflict. Jungleboys are soldiers, stockbrokers, cowboys, and cops. They are boxers, firemen, hockey players, EMTs, ER doctors and outlaws. Truth does not constrain them because they are authentic by nature, unadulterated products of street truth. Their passion and their love for action are real.

Jungle Boy can be a lone hunter or he can travel in a pack. If he travels in a pack, it is because he wants to, not because he needs to. He is effective either way.

3. TradeUp

TradeUp is a spoiled brat who thrives on constant feedback from his entourage. While claiming to be a Republican and a Patriot, he is terrified of being alone and does not truly stand for truth or justice; he knows only how to bask in inherited wealth. Although he may wear a taupe suit with a light blue shirt, he is an Extremist. And he is never wrong. He must have the last word even if he can't pronounce or spell it right in spite of his expensive schooling.

In TradeUp's opinion, his major bargaining chip is money. He is not a self-made man. His success is a function solely of a trust fund, an inheritance or a quid pro quo exchanged for a long-forgotten favor paid in blood by TradeUp's ancestors. (TradeUp's ancestors, by the way, were real men.) TradeUp's spouse will need to bring her own wealth to the table because TradeUp is stingy. He'll clip coupons from the newspaper with tiny little nose scissors so he can cut a precise and perfect line. Or, more frequently, he'll order his personal assistant to do this and other tasks TradeUp considers beneath him (virtually all tasks he can foist off onto someone else). Some TradeUps aren't afraid to marry an ugly girl so long as Mommy approves, but most usually go for Trophy Wife.

TradeUp's relationship with his father was poor, but Mommy always gave him a pass. She bailed him out of those DUIs and went to Al-Anon for him and all, but he's still a mean drunk. At the end of the day it will be you and TradeUp, alone in the living room. With a big fancy bar at the end of the room, and an argument festering in the bottom of his glass at cocktail time. It's five o'clock somewhere.

If you think you can marry TradeUp and not work, you need to redefine "work." Because you will be doing all of TradeUp's dirty work—toting his expensive equipment, cleaning up after him, hopping to at his every whim. Working on a grueling assembly line would be far less demanding than what you'll have to do for this guy. Baking covered dishes for tailgates where you'll freeze your ass off and cleaning up barbeque sauce glued to the back of your new SUV while TradeUp sleeps off his game drunk. You'll have to run the social calendar, or think you're running it, because TradeUp always dreams up events to drag you to without notice. He's very social, and he will expect you to accompany him into the wee hours of the night, while he welcomes in the dawn drinking bloody marys with the same people he blacked out with only hours before. Ever see that toy plastic box from which a frantic voice screams, "Let me outta here!" when you turn it upside down?

TradeUp will constantly nag you to have cosmetic surgery, a boob job or a tummy tuck, while he snorts tubs of buttered lobster. He'll comment constantly about your attire, which will never be perfect enough or expensive enough. He has opinions on everything—even whether your purse "works" with your shoes. Such details are not on Real Man's radar. TradeUp's belief in one primary principle drives his being: that the one with the gold makes the rules. He is brutally racist, classist and superficial. He has never read a novel without first purchasing the CliffsNotes with inherited money.

TradeUp is society's superego, the force that keeps women down, keeps things the way they are and the money where it is. TradeUp never transfers real wealth to a spouse, only a life estate. Real wealth passes by gift, device, or inheritance, man to man.

TradeUp owns guns, maybe even collects them, but he is terrified by them and always makes sure he has all the paperwork. Having the appropriate paperwork is more important to him than actually owning the firearm. We're all for legally required paperwork, but TradeUp is obsessed with it, having gone so far as to frame every FOID card he ever had in chronological order in a gunmetal frame. Keep him out of a uniform and away from guns (with or without paperwork).

Due to his own insecurity, TradeUp cannot survive without an entourage. He is too dependent upon being "popular." In fact, TradeUp is still languishing in Emotional High School, constantly feeding upon the phony adulation of those naive enough to be manipulated by him.

If you throw TradeDown, TradeUp, and Jungle Boy into the ring, Jungle Boy wins. And if you can't stand the thought of waking up next to TradeDown or TradeUp for the rest of your life, why settle for either sad parody of manhood? If you want Jungleboy, and most sane women do, you will need to become as ruthless as he. Because Jungleboy plays rough and he plays hard. He can be as cruel as the jungle that spawned him. The difference between Jungleboy and TradeUp is that TradeUp practices cruelty because he enjoys it, whereas Jungleboy practices it only as needed, to survive. Like the Tiger in *The Life of Pi*, Jungleboy can walk away into the forest and never look back. Don't let him get away.

B. What You Gotta Have Not to Go Nuts

There are certain things you need to be happy. Make a list and add to it as necessary. Here are some sample non-negotiables to get you started:

1. Bathes daily
2. Nonsmoker
3. Financially independent
4. Is a listener and problem solver
5. Can make you laugh, and can laugh at himself

6. Can change a tire, the oil, and his entire personality when this is important to you (and it will be)

7. Can be trusted with keys to your shack

8. Doesn't blab secrets entrusted to him

9. Doesn't calculate sub-totals on smartphone at grocery store

10. Disconnects his technology and listens to your sagas, and after listening, understands and interacts appropriately

11. Doesn't argue every minor point—e.g., whether a cloud is cirrostratus or cirrocumulus (WTF, dude, it's turned into a funnel cloud and HERE IT COMES!)

And now the clincher—how does he treat waiters and waitresses? Or anyone whom he mistakenly perceives as being beneath him in social and/or career status? This tells who he is. A real man need not brandish his power, because others sense it. He does not need the outward trappings of success—fancy cars, trophy wives, big houses. The truly powerful are humble because they recognize that true power emanates not from them, but from a Higher Power.

What kind of tip does he leave? If he leaves less than 18% he's a miser. Know that his generosity toward you will mirror the value of his tip.

Learn to spot the alcoholic. Even a dry drunk is bad news. Does he select only restaurants that serve booze? How does he react when you suggest a restaurant without a wine list?

No slime balls allowed. Those creepy guys who wear too much cologne and still smell bad. Reptiles who sit too closely when they have just met you. Those smarmy ones, not Johnny Depp pirate smarmy, but those who coil in dark corners. You can identify them by their teeth, exposed too long when feigning smiles. They use phrases like "hook up." They try to get their child support lowered. They slither up alongside you before you realize they're there. Be vigilant and trust your instincts. These snakes are not above dropping a surprise tablet in your drink. They were sent by The Enemy to corrupt and destroy you and to mock your dreams.

Prospect needs to own up to any criminal record right from the get-go. And get it straight whether he packs heat. If he gets locked up, it may be difficult for you to find time to go visit him on a regular basis. And putting money on his books can quickly get old, as does the view from six feet under if he gets out of hand with that sawed-off shotgun he failed to mention. Put your safety first.

You may have totally different non-negotiables—age, fitness, health, height, hair color, or educational level. You don't want Santa Claus, nor do you want Peter Pan. You want someone who feels lucky to be with you. Someone who treasures you and hangs on your every word even though that means he sometimes smothers you. He'll put you first. Even if he has serial affairs, his emotional loyalty is unquestionable. You can kick his ass to the curb when he does stray, but rest assured he'll feel genuine remorse once reality kicks in and he realizes it's over.

VI

Online Dating: A Search for the Truth

A. His Profile

1. Read between the Lines

If his top athletic interest is shooting pool, you can bet your last Bud he's drinking more than a few beers while he's out doing it. And if he's 55 and never been married, chances are he's immature, selfish, or just plain can't maintain a relationship because he doesn't have the people skills or the commitment to anyone or anything other than his own face in the mirror. He is either plagued by childish indecision, or he has not yet learned to put others first. Leave him to languish on the Island of Lost Boys.

2. Photos

If he has posted 200 pictures of himself in every possible pose, he's got too much time on his hands. He will continue surfing the online dating sites long after you make the mistake of becoming an item with him. Beware of online daters who have posted the same pictures for three years, or who have been on a site more than a few months. And BTW, why have you been on there long enough to know that?

Consider it more than a little odd when he posts photos of himself in front of a messy, unmade bed. There's a difference between cute and sloppy. Beware as well of the too-perfect photo. Skin too smooth, abs too tight, too many model-like poses. Keep looking.

Pray tell what is it with the facial hair and the motorcycles? What is manly about a two-ton machine between one's legs? Is it manly to be hurled, unhelmeted, into the oblivion of a traumatic brain injury? To be scraped off of the highway by the EMTs? You don't have time to be risking life and limb on some windblown motorcycle ride through Deliverance County. Unless you love biking enough to risk having a family member summoned to the morgue to ID your body. Its risk can be a draw. Understanding and acknowledging risk will either help you avoid it or draw you to it even more powerfully. If you go, wear a helmet. If you recognize on that first ride that he is an unsafe driver, and you're lucky enough to get a second chance, Just Say No.

3. I versus You

Count the number of times he uses "I," "me," and "you." This is not rocket science. Some believe that dating sites are like catalogs that offer whatever configuration of characteristics they can conjure up. His profile length tells the story—no subject is more fascinating than oneself, or more boring to others.

Look for the "we's." The word can smother you before you even meet him. You do want to know which outdoor activities he will insist that you attend—football games, for instance, or long boring afternoons playing that sport-that-is-not-a-sport. If you love those sports, then be glad to see, "We'll tailgate before the game." Also look for the sometimes telling absence of "we's." If he mentions interest in sports but doesn't include the reader in the picture, he may be planning to use those activities as an excuse to drink with the boys or cavort with other women.

4. Smoking

"Smoke but 'trying' to quit," means he recognizes that smoking is probably a turnoff; it does *not* mean that he's actually trying to quit. When someone says "I'll try to make it," they won't be there. But if you are a smoker (God help you) and are also looking for one, then give him points for honesty and for at least knowing that it's politically correct to be making an effort to quit.

5. Income

This one's simple. If his profile states that the woman he dates must earn a certain amount of income per year, he's either a gigolo or a miser. Your earnings are nobody's business but yours, your accountant's and the IRS's. Such a requirement may reflect a doglike guarding of resources. This reptile will demand an airtight prenup. Which is no skin off your nose because you want one too, to his astonishment. But unlike him, you have vision, plans and a financial future. A man who decides to date you based upon your earnings record may be planning on tapping into your retirement. Even if he does have a sizeable IRA, don't count on being the beneficiary. His ex may have obtained an interest in his IRA in their divorce. He may not disclose his holdings, or any liens on them. Rely only on your own lien-free assets and your own two hands. Obtain legal advice before signing any legal documents, including prenups.

Learn to spot generosity. Animal lovers tend to be caring and nurturing, particularly if they are involved in rescue organizations. Does his "community service" ring true, or was it part of a criminal justice sentence? A corporate insider on the board of a charitable organization is probably only doing it to beef up his own paltry resume, line his own coffers, or snag a promotion. This is not true charity. True charity requires sacrifice. It has to hurt.

6. Marital Status

Potential partners will come to you with baggage—either a deceased or a divorced spouse, or lifelong bachelorhood. There is a tendency to be more open and accepting at this stage of your life, due in part to the abundant empathy and wisdom gained through your own loss. But choose carefully.

a. Separated. The newly separated are problematic on a variety of levels. Disclosing the "separated" status counts for something. But reconciliation is often cheaper than divorce, and reconcile they may, and just when you least expect it. In fact, they may not be separated at all.

b. Divorced. At sixty, he might be done paying alimony and child support, but his adult children may fight you for what little he has left. If you happen to be a lawyer, ascertain whether he is trying to connect with you just to get free legal service so he can wage an ongoing war with his ex.

There are many reasons for divorce—some defensible, others not. You need to find out why. Use his online language as a springboard for your investigation. Information you learn in online searches is sometimes outdated or intentionally misleading. But start there and find out as much about the person as possible. Then hire the Rolls Royce of investigators, one who follows all ethical rules. Spend the money. And don't argue with the investigator's findings even if you'd rather not believe them. You hired the best for a reason. Unless you want to spend your hard-earned emotional independence and cash supporting a deadbeat and pretending not to see his lapses or your own bruises, trust your gut and your investigator.

If he divorced due to infidelity, either his former spouse's or his own, you might decide to give him a pass. If the infidelity occurred during his midlife crisis, it may have been situational. Then again, he may be taking meds long-term, and driven by the modern-day Power Couple—Viagra and male menopause.

There are usually at least two reasons why a marriage ends— the real reason and the fake one. It's the same phenomenon in employment termination. The employer fabricates the fake reason to avoid a lawsuit—for instance, refusal to "be a team player." The true reason is usually grainier and more interesting—refusal of the boss's advances, for example. In assessing the divorced male, evaluate the acceptability of the reason he provides according to how and when he discloses it, how he describes it, and the level of rage with which it has left him. He has to be willing to genuinely acknowledge his own fault. If he hasn't let it go, you'll be married to both him and his shadow. Three's a crowd.

c. Widowed. Widowers are an interesting breed. They are often snapped up quickly because, like dazed prey, they are still paralyzed by grief. Be prepared to be compared. Reach a reasonable understanding about pictures of the deceased significant other and memorabilia from the prior relationship. Look for someone with an open mind who respects that you and your family want to honor your previous spouse on certain occasions. And respect Prospect's desire to do so as well.

If on the other hand you or he has a shrine to the deceased in every room, it may not be time to move forward. *And that's okay.* Don't apologize for your decision to remain single—for now or forever. You may decide you have more to offer the world without entanglements with people who cannot, even in their wildest dreams, measure up to your deceased spouse. Move forward with everything that your soul mate left you— the confidence, the self-esteem, the drive and the power. And if he left you with none of these, now is your time to develop such qualities with guidance and support from spiritual mentors, friends, family and colleagues. Ask for their input and suggestions; your true supporters will be happy to help you emerge from the fire unscathed and empowered. Keep an open mind and believe that all things are possible and that anyone (2- or 4-leggers!) can be the source of great inspiration and companionship.

Your own marital status is less important than whether you have come to grips with it. Knowing whether you're ready to seek a partner can be a difficult decision fraught with elusive and surprising emotions. One day you may be ready, and the next day overcome by embarrassment about being on an online dating site at all. You'd feel every bit as exposed in a bar or on a singles cruise. You probably didn't feel that way in the Sixties because well, they were the Sixties after all and who the hell remembers. But be guided by the spirit of the Sixties—follow your heart to a quiet place where you can ponder what is best for you.

7. Location

The difficulty of maintaining a long-distance relationship increases the probability that the partners continue to "shop" for something closer to home. So, bear this in mind when defining the parameters of your online search.

Some online seekers enumerate a laundry list of their residences over the past years, perhaps to make themselves appear more cosmopolitan and worldly. After all, who could resist the amorous advances of a man who spent the summer in Paris . . . Illinois? More often, however, multiple successive hometowns can be a red flag signaling instability or legal entanglements.

If he's right in your own backyard, prepare to be bored. To tears. But at least you'll know where he's coming from. If he lives more than 30 miles away, let him come to your town (not to your home). Any man who expects you to drive back and forth to and from his hometown is lazy and undeserving of your time unless his sole reason for not making the trip is that he is physically unable or has demanding caretaking commitments.

Disregard anyone whose profile says he's not willing to relocate, unless there's a good reason—elderly family members, financial concerns or family ties. But if he's just that guy who's enslaved by his past and by his paltry real-estate holdings, recognize his inflexibility as a red flag. You don't want someone who expects you to do all the uprooting and settle into whatever arbitrary and capricious routine he dictates. A blanket refusal ever to relocate speaks volumes. Leave him to unhitch his pony and play with it in the OK Corral known as his Own Back Yard. Until the bank forecloses, in which case, Cowgirl, he'd be more than willing to modify his previous non-relocation policy, pack up his lasso, and move in with you—but for the fact that you will have already screened him out of the running if you have heeded this warning.

8. Employment

Retired men who haven't opted to be involved in meaningful pursuits, interests, passions or callings have too much free time. If he's there champing at the bit to be involved in every nano-decision that you make and wanting to take expensive, lengthy vacations when you have things to do and ambitions to pursue, conflict ensues.

Pay no heed to rich people with fat retirement plans just waiting for a certain age when they can finally stop doing what they've hated doing all these years. They will glamorize retirement and for them, because they have found their careers so distasteful, retirement will indeed be nirvana. Of course, if you want to retire and can still follow your calling while being retired, then pursue that dream. But don't do it because you are persuaded by the retirees' swan songs of monthly pension plans from corporations who sucked them dry of life. Do it when the time is right for you, when you decide to become who you were meant to be.

Everyone knows the basic characteristics of most professionals. To recap, however, and help you keep your radar tuned to a variety of frequencies and rule out undesirables, here are just a few (of course, there are exceptions within each category):

a. **Accountant:** Brilliant and wealthy, but unavailable during tax season.
b. **Artist:** A keeper, if you are independently wealthy and can support him. Will cherish your free spirit.
c. **Auctioneer:** Do we even have to say it?
d. **Doctor:** Perfectionist, either perfectly arrogant or perfectly compassionate. Works long hours and is rarely home.
e. **Engineer:** As boring as science itself.
f. **Financial Analyst:** Great at assessing stocks, people and life.
g. **Funeral Director:** Kind and understanding. An A+ for him.

h. Lawyer: If you find a True Lawyer—one who fiercely guards the integrity of the Constitution and who practices law in the real world with real clients—take him on.

i. Psychologist: Interesting, kind and helpful. You could drink a beer with him, possibly gaining remarkable insight into your problems in the process.

j. Social Worker: Has a heart, a soul, and a sincere mission. Outstanding listener, mediator and problem solver.

k. Substance Abuse Counselor: Gets it and gets life and people. Accepts but does not enable imperfections. Believes in human potential.

l. Truck Driver: Just Say No, unless you really love being on your own. He's never home.

m. Veterinarian: A keeper.

Which other professions and careers come to mind? Pick one or two and summarize them in a couple of words. Here are just a few to get you started:

Airline Pilot_____

_____

Basketball Coach_____

_____

Computer Programmer_____

_____

Factory Worker_____

_____

FBI Agent_____

_____

High School Principal_____

_____

Hotel Manager_____

_____

IT Expert_____

_____

Judge_____

_____

Landscaper_____

_____

U.S. Marine_____

_____

Other_____

_____

Get a man who works at something. There is so much out there to do—crafts, skiing, tennis, various philanthropic organizations that do great things. Work that's worth doing. Men who don't work have too much time to fix their hair, worry about how short they are, or camp out on online dating sites looking for Miss Goodbooby. Retirees who don't engage in meaningful callings expect too much of you. Even if you have left your own career behind, or are considering doing so, they should not be on your short list. Why? Because there aren't enough hours in the day for us to do our own bodily maintenance, pursue our interests, and then come home only to be dragged to some ridiculous canned activity with someone who's had the whole day to catch up on his naps so he'll have evenings free to make a fool of himself pursuing the butterfly of youth.

Real men work real man jobs. They move things forward. They work construction, sales, or own their own businesses. Steer clear of men who spend too much time at flea markets or are obsessed with getting a set paycheck and following a corporate chain of command. You can bet your booty this same man wants to be at the top of the little corporation he's planning on forming with you. You on the other hand, may forever remain tied to the bottom rung of his jealously guarded corporate ladder. If you like leaders, pick a true leader. Only the powerful can lead the powerful. Some real men have a crowd of people around them because they are loved and revered. These men are popular, but they don't seek popularity. They don't speak often but when they do, they have something to say. They use short, succinct sentences to explain both complex and simple concepts. The flowerier the phrase, the wimpier the man. Real men take chances and make decisions. They are not fearful of challengers.

9. Too Many Demands

Beware of the "no baggage" request in online profiles. Baggage per se is not objectionable. We all carry some. One seeking a woman without a past may have a shady one himself. What is important is how we deal with it—do we have sense enough to check all our bags sometimes, or do we insist on dragging around too many carry-ons? Do our bags routinely pop open without notice due to defective zippers? Are the wheels on our suitcases broken or wobbly? Pack your baggage properly so you can carry it with ease. And avoid assuming responsibility for others' baggage; managing your own may be all you can handle at least during your transition.

Also to be avoided are people who issue directives in their profiles. You don't want control freaks or bullies. Run like the wind from a person whose profile states in all caps, "DO NOT REPLY IF YOU ARE OFFENDED BY THIS PROFILE." Of course you're not going to reply, but this E-Shouter must have the last word. He is criticism-proof. He has been hurt and hurt badly, and he doesn't want to talk about it. This lack of self-awareness will drive him even further toward the edge of his spectrum. Don't try to straighten him out online. It's too time-consuming a task and will only generate hostile responses while wasting your own precious minutes.

10. Drinking

Some Reptiles foolishly post photos of themselves with red noses. Take heed. Also look carefully at his favorite restaurants—is their only common denominator the fact that they serve booze? And how much wine country is really out there to explore, after all? If you don't drink, maybe you don't mind being the designated driver. But wine country is usually in hilly areas with winding roads, and wine aficionados who have over-imbibed might be out there behind the wheel. Beware, too, of the man who lays it right out there that he needs a lot of alone time or travels a lot. These habits may be camouflaging unexplained benders, serial love fests or something far more sinister.

11. Dining

If his favorite dish is anything with arugula, keep looking. No real man even knows what arugula is. Real men eat meat and potatoes, and pieces of chocolate cake the size of Nevada. Real men like cheeseburgers and Ho-Hos. No man wants you to be constantly dieting and harping about what you can't have. Like hunching over your phone during a date, your refusal to man up and order real food can disengage you from the dining experience you are sharing (unless medical dietary considerations have become an unnoticed part of your life, and your potential suitor has the wisdom and understanding to respect without belaboring these restrictions). You can complain about your dietary restrictions if you occasionally need to vent, but don't make a career of it. Unless of course you have health-related restrictions and it helps you to talk about them privately with Prospect and with treasured members of your inner circle who want only the best for you. Prospect's willingness or lack thereof, to listen in such cases is another great litmus test of your compatibility.

Beware of men wannabes who stray too far from the four basic food groups: meat, chocolate, dairy, and salty. If he orders a twist cone at the local ice cream shack, it had better be straight vanilla or chocolate, not a random fruity concoction with a frilly name. And if he orders a small cone, call it a day. No real man has ever ordered a small cone. Or a veggie wrap. Say what? The end is near, or should be.

Ultimately his culinary preferences are inconsequential, so long as he shuts the hell up about them. He can be a vegetarian if he's doing it for the right reasons, such as health, the environment or not wanting to eat anything that has ever had a face. But if he's doing it because he thinks it's fashionable, you're done. It's about authenticity, and there are many authentic, acceptable reasons to not eat certain foods. Political correctness is not one of them.

And don't let him make you cook in his ridiculous, gas-hogging RV. That is not a vacation for anyone except him, as you will be doing all the "housework." In fact, anyone with the phrase "RV" in his profile needs to hop into it and hit the long-and-winding road. And may the wind be always at his back so he doesn't waste so damn much gasoline. Guess who gets to clean it out at the end of a 3-week "adventure."

12. Beware of the "Shoulds"!

"Should" is a big word. The person who uses it is usually judgmental, critical, and arrogant. He sits back and solves others' problems, rarely addressing his own. My mother has always said that most of us are quite good at solving others' problems. Mr. Should will be the first to tell you he is far better at solving your problems than you are. Count the number of times "should" appears in his profile: "The woman I am looking for *should* love to travel." First of all, love cannot be created on command. Mr. Should will not be able to accept your genuine emotions and will try to manipulate and control your feelings. He is incapable of agreeable disagreement. He will micromanage you and you will have no say in how you spend Sunday afternoons.

13. Music

Musical preferences speak volumes. If he likes country he may have rural roots or want to connect with basic values such as honesty, simplicity and loyalty. Then again, he may just love beer and barbeque and there are worse things.

Amazingly, many online daters make a huge point of saying they don't like rap music. Okay, so now you know who they are. As in any genre, there are great and not so great beats. You can't dictate someone else's preferences, but blanket contempt for an entire musical genre may suggest other prejudices and inflexibilities.

If he likes Bob Dylan or Bob Marley, he could be an old hippie or a tree hugger embracing a liberal lifestyle due to its perceived fashionability. On the other hand, he may just appreciate authentic talent. Beware of anyone who is too serious a fan of any individual musician or group, as these fans either have insufficient self-esteem or are borderline cultists. Has he devoted his life to acquiring memorabilia of a certain star, for instance? This could mean he likes to waste weekends at flea markets or garage sales. You don't have time for that.

We all have our yellow brick roads to be sure, but beware of obsession in any form.

Your Elvis fan is a horse of another color. He may not admit his passion on a dating site, but mentioning Memphis as a favorite hotspot is a sign. This could also mean he's grossly overweight from porking out on Q or peanut butter and banana sandwiches. But if a man puts a notch on his concealed carry holster every time he visits Graceland, go along and enjoy the ride.

And a little about musicians. Aside from the reputed alcohol and drug propensities and the iron-fisted influence fellow band members wield over his lifestyle, the bottom line is that he'll be staying out late. Probably in his own garage or some Grade-B venue. You could tag along on his gigs, but this will become tedious and maybe even dangerous. Bar parking lots are a risky business after the bouncers have bounced into their red Ford pickups and headed for after-hours bars with bouncers even bigger than they are.

True musicians are to be revered. Anyone who has ever heard great guitar knows just how nimble and artistic bony fingers can be. The only thing more fun than hearing Keith Richards playing the guitar is listening to his interviews—the cigarette, the knowing smile, the totally charming lack of respect. You sense that he's visualizing the next guitar riff while simultaneously engaging in amusing interview banter. If you're planning on hooking up with a real musician, know one thing: We can't stay up as late now as we did in the Sixties. We might wake up at 4:00 regardless of when we retired the night before. To get enough sleep we have to frontload it. For this reason, musicians can pose a health risk. But there's no sweeter sound than your man singing to you in a crowded room as the other bitches long for him.

The man who listens solely to blues and jazz may be either a phony or really, really depressed. You can't sing along to this music. Newsflash: the band's about to go on its final break and we have to dance while we can. Spend your time with the chronically upbeat, maybe with a little flash of the dark side on special occasions.

14. Clothes

It's frightening how many men post photos in which they are wearing a T-shirts with the head hole stretched out. Are they *trying* to look bummy? Hoping people will like them for themselves? We don't need a tux, but at least wear a T-shirt that doesn't look like it was washed, if at all, on a pioneer-era washboard.

Or better yet—the T-shirt TUCKED IN with a tight belt. If he had someone around to direct how he dressed, there might be hope. But the question is, do you want to be that person? To waste your precious time and breath whining at the man about his clothes, and then waiting around while he changes into something equally ridiculous? Ultimately, such drama will strain your relationship.

And now to Tuxwearer—the man who overdresses for his profile photo. He is every bit as sad as Guy-with-Head-Punched-Out-T-Shirt. Tuxwearer's apparent discomfort makes it obvious that this is not his normal attire. He is also likely to post a ten-year-old photo—the last time he wore a tux—perhaps from his daughter's wedding if he was allowed in. No doubt his tux and accessories are made of cheap materials—and, a closer glance reveals, in need of a good ironing.

Yet another breed of the two-legged beast posts an array of photos of himself in a variety of costumes, from tux to the tiara when he dressed as Snow White for Halloween. This is apparently to demonstrate that he is as in touch with his formal as he is with his feminine side. Instead of demonstrating flexibility, these photos show lack of spine. He will follow each new trend and friend to the end of time, always seeking popularity at the cost of all else. Plus, who cares if he surfboards and plays chess at the same time. He's searching for something and it isn't you.

15. Self–Serving Characterizations

Treatises could be written about the rampant self-serving statements in profiles. Probably three-fourths of the profiles profess that the male seeker is "romantic." The "romantic" are usually in the throes of midlife crises, late-onset or otherwise, seeking something they can't define.

Representatives of certain professions consider themselves "articulate," but be particularly aware of the charlatan in sheep's clothes. Con artists in a variety of professions who bend the English language to serve their basest needs are the most dangerous predators of all. Don't allow them to prey upon your fears; chances are that any victories they claim to have won pale in comparison to your own triumph over loss and your determination to prevail in future battles.

These self-serving statements are helpful though, since the predator's professed areas of strength reveal his greatest weaknesses. Perhaps he read an online article about "How to Write a Profile," an article he interpreted to mean that all women want romance. The "Tell the Truth" memo, however, apparently went directly to his spam folder, bypassing what's left of his cerebellum. Read between the lines--the predator's most terrifying instincts lie in wait beneath the surface.

Class, like pornography, is difficult to define—but you know it when you see it. Anyone who refers to himself as "classy," isn't. Just as old money does not speak of itself, the classy elite don't mention their own classiness. This trait must be perceived naturally by others, and it must be based upon truth, not manipulative self-promotion. The truly classy are humble, and they are wise. They don't tell you what you "should" do, because their innate classiness compels them to respect you enough to trust that you can handle yourself on your own. They don't tell you where to sit in social situations because they know that you know where to sit. And if in the slim chance you don't, and you land somewhere other than the "right" place, the truly classy do not judge, but rather, they defend you. When they offer to help, the offer is specific and sincere.

Some of these Truly Classy swam out to your little island in Chaos Sea to help you when your soul mate died—offered to help you move, sell your house, pack. They followed through.

Some of the Unclassy also washed up onshore, wringing their hands and asking, "Is there anything I can do?" *Bring him back from the dead*, you thought. But sometimes poor class is not intentional. If they bothered to show up for the funeral or to contact you in the gale of the hurricane, give them a pass. They may just never have been brought up to know what to say. But they made the effort.

B. Your Profile

1. Be Truthful

This isn't a confession, but don't be afraid to mention a weakness or two. And don't tout your weaknesses as badges of honor ("I'm a workaholic," "shopaholic," etc.). No real Prospect wants to hear how much disposable income you have or how high-maintenance you are. Bragging about your wealth will generally make you quite unpopular with everyone but the gigolo set.

Truth is imperative. The rage and pain when lies are uncovered will undermine any potential relationship. This does not mean, however, that you are required to answer Predator's overly personal questions. This isn't a Q&A for his entertainment. There will be time later for meaningful conversation, not with Predator of course, but with those worthy of your time.

2. Know Your Value

If respecting yourself turns off certain macho control freak bully types, your newly acquired self-confidence is doing its job. Good riddance. Failure to convey your sense of self-worth is fatal to your quest for someone who cares about you, treasures you and puts you first. Being succinct and professional, yet kind and flexible, will convey your self-esteem. Apologize for nothing, and don't end sentences with "I think" or stick too many qualifiers into every sentence. Such words convey weakness and insecurity, if overused.

3. PLEASE Get to the Point

As Elvis once sang, "A little less conversation, a little more action, please." One rationale for online dating is that it can save time. Remember this as you write your profile—don't mindlessly meander into personal details ad nauseam. Although disclosing your exact dating goals would theoretically save everyone's time, some of the old ways are still appropriate. You wouldn't dream of blurting out on a first date that you are seeking a man who will stay home and help babysit your grandchildren while you gallivant the globe practicing international law. And you would likely have serious concerns about someone who probed too deeply into your psyche on a first date. Getting to truly know someone can take time as layers of the human mask are gently exfoliated. And yet, sometimes veracity can unexpectedly be revealed by quick, spontaneous bursts of real-time conversation, which is why there is no substitute for it. Because predators disclose only those personas they want you to see, any information they provide online may not be reliable. Look into his eyes (in a public place), read his facial microexpressions, and trust your gut.

More important than enumerating a checklist of "what you are seeking," is stating who you are, where you are coming from and where you are going (with or without him). Be concise, and don't be unreasonably specific. Men who might otherwise have been interested in you will head for the hills when they see a checklist of twenty detailed characteristics and interests, only 3 of which match their own preferences.

And this should be true for your personal attitude toward online dating as well: too many non-negotiables can entrap you in a virtual world where you are left chasing the Holy Grail into perpetuity. Quit wondering whether there is someone out there with that one more thing you want. There probably is. But that person will have other flaws that didn't occur to you when you began this journey.

Present your best argument first. Don't meander on about romance and waves lapping up onto shores. They've heard it before and clichés make you look unoriginal and boring.

Part of the internet's allure is its illusion of an enormous quantity of *viable* fish in the sea. This fantasy drives many online daters to check every category in the e-questionnaire that arguably demonstrates youth and savvy. Don't make that mistake. Don't check "love to go clubbing" unless you really do. Checking too many boxes telegraphs weakness. You are not fishing for minnows. You're after a Great White, a man who's powerful, confident, and ruthless in his commitment to action, to survival and to life, and yet no match for you.

So, get to the point, and don't get to too many points or your message will be no more than a note in a bottle cast out to sea. Break up any narratives into short sentences and short paragraphs. Just the facts, ma'am.

4. Photos

The photos you choose should reflect who you are on a good day. Don't photoshop your pictures to make yourself look younger. Your honesty will weed out the superficial two-legger who is relentlessly pursuing a decades-younger woman, a pursuit that sometimes ends badly.

Do wear a color that flatters, but nothing too cheap, tight or sparkly. On the other hand, times have changed since the long flowing skirts of the Sixties. You're not 25, but if you're well preserved there is no need to hide behind layers of clothing, droopy hats, or cars you wish were yours.

Don't post 25 pictures. The male attention span is short. Post one face shot (gazing up into the camera) and a full shot to illustrate that you do not weigh 350. A common misconception of men is that any woman who doesn't post a full-body shot weighs 350. Ironically, the vast majority of men who whine about this through yellow teeth so often resemble an overweight Father Time.

5. Be Flexible

Don't compromise on what you need. Chemistry, for instance. But take a long hard look at your must-haves. Does it really matter, for instance, if he is only 5'11" as opposed to 6', if the taller guy smokes? Try to see the big picture.

Prioritize three to five things you think you must have. For instance: 1) nonsmoker; 2) gainfully employed; 3) 210 pounds max; 4) college degree. But don't pretend to be flexible on an issue that is really a non-negotiable. You will waste your time and Prospect's. You don't have time to waste.

Keep an open mind. The human brain is complex. If vision is lost, hearing sharpens. If you find a man whose big picture fills your bill on your primary non-negotiables, you may be able to overlook some details. (Though bear in mind that if you are planning to "fix" him once you're married, this is likely to be even more difficult now that both of you are older, as habits may be more indelibly ingrained.) But avoid the desperate. Many online daters are not only imperfect, they are painfully lonely, like a lone man standing in front of brightly colored wrinkled curtains hung to create the illusion of a window in a dark basement.

Determining your physical non-negotiables is not difficult. You know, for instance, what height, weight, and complexion range you usually find attractive. The operative word is "range." Go into a dating site, pick out pictures of men you find physically attractive and notice the degree of variation in their basic features. Consider the variety of people you dated prior to your soul mate. This will expand your mind and increase your flexibility.

Seeking and finding a clone of your departed Übermensch will not heal the pain and may even increase it. Don't rate your prospects according to whether their features mirror your soul mate's. Slowly but surely small dissimilarities will appear. These disparities will be mildly annoying at first, then crescendo into full-blown disgust which forces you to re-experience the pain of loss. Keep your soul mate's memory pure in your heart, untainted with replicas who will always fall short, like fake Guccis or low-fat cottage cheese.

Your soul mate is gone. It has been hell to deal with, but you can't go back. He can never truly die; you loved him too much. But now is the time to free your mind, to clear out the clutter so you can decide whether to go it alone for a while or forever, or to get back out in the fray. Your call.

Ideas about where to meet people, how to act, and how to adjust are probably already occurring to you. Develop them, brainstorm about them. Make lists and plans. You have already adjusted many aspects of your life in order to survive. The remaining adjustments will follow, if you keep working and evolving. Take a moment now to start this process by writing down one or two places where you would feel comfortable meeting men (even if just a little outside your comfort zone):

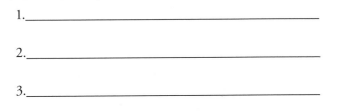

1._____

2._____

3._____

VII

Your Dating Database

There are as many dating resources and strategies as there are fish in the sea. The only hard and fast rules are: 1) be a player, not a spectator; and 2) be willing to get out of your comfort zone. Following those two rules will increase your dating pool and therefore, your odds.

A. Married People and Families

Avoid most married couples. They can be really annoying. Their wives don't want you around for fear you will steal their hard-won "prizes." They will exclude you from conversation and make you feel awkward and uncomfortable, so leave them to their own feeble devices—watching TV every night or engaging in tiresome routines. Disabuse yourself of the notion that these boring codependents will ever help you find someone who's truly worth dating. At best, you will provide gossip fodder at their couples-based events. Remember, "Insecure people only eclipse your sun because they're jealous of your daylight and tired of their dark, starless nights."[4]

Married women hate single women, even when the single women are old, fat, and broke. We represent freedom and autonomy they will never have. But more importantly, they are afraid we will try to steal their husbands. It would be highly advisable for these married women to take a quick glance at that hubby. When was the last time a woman, other than a waitress who flirts for tips, bothered to look his way?

Sometimes you can't help but feel some bitterness as you watch nuclear families pile into expensive jeeps or take up the whole row of a 747. Recognize and accept this feeling as part of grief anger. The happy families are oblivious to the future, to the loss that they will experience when nature takes its course. You envy their obliviousness. This phenomenon occurs more frequently when you are in a confined space, and when you happen to be totally alone. Everything is magnified, including your emotions. These moments can be devastating. Allow yourself a brief flash of sadness or anger. Putting a reasonable time limit on it helps it pass. Bitter can sometimes make you better; a short episode of anger or resentment can spawn a long overdue epiphany or spiritual metamorphosis. Just dust yourself off, change your venue, and enjoy a sunlit day, a favorite tune, or the current *National Enquirer.*

Do tell your married friends that you are on the market if you are. Because they are just as bored as they are boring, they may pass this along—and to be candid, you need all the marketing you can get. Awkward social events where you and some lizard like "single" man are the only unattached people are off limits. But do put the word out there.

---

[4] Shannon L. Alder, author

B. Online

Join the sites. Pay up. Being hurt on an online dating site is a unique kind of pain. Be prepared for this novel twist of agony. But the better moments boost you up. Even an online flirtation from someone you're not interested in can boost the ego and kick you into high gear on a blue Monday. But don't just collect unwanted winks like antiques, saving them in your inbox for future reference or for an ego boost. Pitch them. At sixty you have no time to waste on stagnant messages from those who did not survive your initial cut.

C. Old Flame

High school reunions can be sad gatherings. The newly wrinkled standing at watering holes trying to be somebody, fueled by alcohol and delusion. But maybe there's something left unsaid, an unanswered question. Look through the photos of your classmates in your high school yearbook. But don't ask around about someone you're interested in. Let him find you. Because if he is interested, you hunting him down like a lion stalks a wildebeest will only cause him to surround himself with his own kind, keeping your desperation at bay. You alone have the power to let him man up. Use it wisely.

How, then, should you let Old Flame know you are available—if you want to be found, that is? (And there are days when you don't, we get that.) Gazing out the window from your recliner probably won't call Prospect forth no matter how many times you chant "abracadabra." Part of your job is simple—be findable.

Doing something that you love passionately will make you findable, not just to Old Flame but to New Flame(s) as well. Get involved in a religious organization, a political campaign, or a charitable cause. Animal rescue organizations often need volunteers. Be more than an online presence for these causes. Merely having your email address on an organization's listserv will not usually result in new friendships or relationships, so ask to be appointed to a committee or nominated as an officer. Develop a project that will help an organization and approach its representative with your vision. Then work and cooperate with the team assigned to the project, being careful to gain the consensus and mutual commitment that will move the project forward. Listen and consider ideas that differ from yours and be flexible so that the project evolves in the organization's best interest. Be sure that your fellow committee or project members are appreciated. Always offer thanks and compliments for great ideas and jobs well done. Don't make it about meeting men, but about getting others on board to achieve a goal that is important to you. The ties, friendships and relationships with those who share your vision will follow. As an added bonus, you can add these activities to your resume.

Being findable before you're ready, or to the wrong people, has potential hazards. Exercise caution as you enter your social media settings. You may be more comfortable with paid than unpaid dating sites, but there are plenty of bad people out there who can afford to drop thirty bucks a month to harass women online. And it may not be financially feasible now for you to pay for online dating. Regardless of your social media settings or your online dating participation, don't disclose your phone number to anyone you meet online until you've developed a good sense of where the person is coming from using the judgment, wisdom and common sense that you've gained over the years.

As for Old Flame, he probably still hangs out where he always did. Old flames are tired, old, and predictable, but they are usually reliable, a characteristic that becomes more important as time goes by. Who will take you to the ER when you have a TIA? Will he be playing pool, too drunk to walk, or off working on an oil rig in Timbuktu? Will he listen to you when you get the crazies? And the crazies will come, sometimes spewing forth unpredictably from the ashes of loss.

And listening doesn't mean "straightening you out"—it means appreciating all of your idiosyncrasies and occasional lapses from convention. It can't bother him that you like modern art or that your own art projects are based upon surreal concepts. Old Flame may well have a tough time accepting your many dimensions; only you know whether he's worth taking a shot.

The primary problem with Old Flame is simply this: he didn't step up to the plate before, and he probably hasn't grown a pair in the past 40 years. People don't usually change, they just become more of the same.

But if the chemistry is still there, and he's single (leave the married ones married)—interest him by being interesting. Find things to talk about other than your job or your grandkids. Be interested—in the other person, the past, the future, and most importantly, in the present. Treat the present moment like a long-lost love. Perhaps through your example, Old Flame will learn to rekindle his own spark, and you two can share a "Happily Ever After." But to be candid, things didn't work out before and the odds are against him. Remember, however, that basing all action on probability can be confining and send you into a dizzying tailspin--precious moments, hours and years are voraciously consumed as you weigh the odds into perpetuity.

D. Fix-Ups by Friends

Get a picture. And find out what kind of voice he has. You can tell by looking at a picture whether he's city or country—the eyes, dress, and demeanor give it away. City Boy knows how to run from a knife and duck from a gun. He can fight because he's had to. He can cuss because he's had to. And he may kick you to the curb just because he can. Don't agree to a fix-up without a photograph. If you don't get one, make an excuse. Any excuse. Maybe you need to go to target practice. Or to St. Louis to get magenta hair extensions.

Run an online background check on the man. Best $39.95 you will have ever spent.

Keep your personal life personal. Your dreams are yours—keep them close to your heart. Don't let the unworthy probe into them to gain an edge. You can disclose what needs to be disclosed in good time.

VIII

Communication—How and When to Email or Text

A. Email or E-Jail

Hunching over a computer and reading emails is not living. You may have to tolerate your computer's bullying during work hours—few of us have the luxury of never sitting tethered to a desk and staring at a monitor until our eyes glaze over like we're Children of the Corn. But the inbox can be addictive—the sparkle of the ads and new colors, animations of clearing faces advertising expensive face creams. The sense of being totally on top of things, in control. (If ever you doubt this, uninstall a program just because you can, then reinstall it.) Addiction to electric shadows is powerful indeed.

If your computer brings you joy, savor it wisely, like fine chocolate. But don't let it ensnare you to the exclusion of real relationships and important spiritual connections such as those that strengthened your bond with Soul Mate when you first met, and which will help you overcome future challenges.

We all have—or hope or pretend to have—that certain someone from whom we eagerly await an email. The anticipation we experience for the next missive fluctuates in direct proportion to the length and frequency of the incomings—the shorter and more succinct the message, the more unpredictable its arrival time, the more eagerly we await the next.

One potential downfall of email is that it can be tailored, sculpted, proofread, and revised. Each revision can excise a piece of soul, and more skillfully obfuscate the truth. The right time will come for emailing to take a back seat to a real relationship. Hiding under cover of cyberspace can be comforting, but you are more than a pen pal. Email can begin and end a relationship, but it cannot sustain one. It can only sustain addiction to itself.

When do you kick it up a notch? A real man will take the lead. But now in your sixties, you don't have time to wait around for someone to man up, so don't be shy. A phone call can reveal truths easily masked in email communications. We want the phone call to mean something, and our desires fulfill that prophecy. If he can't commit to picking up the phone, he isn't interested or he isn't who he says he is. He may be keeping you on hold in case nothing "better" turns up. These monitor mannequins navigate their keyboards more artfully than Sulu piloted the *Starship Enterprise*. And they feel just as powerful, launching through cyberspace at sobering speeds. They are, after all, just trying to be somebody.

So, don't let email become e-jail. If you are serious about finding your soul mate, give yourself an ultimatum. Pick the time frame, but if you're hovering on the cusp of shorter or longer, opt for shorter. If he hasn't upped the ante after one week by trying to meet you in person, delete him. Listen carefully to the click each time you open a message from Prospect. Because each such click is just one more tick of the time bomb signaling the end—if you can call it an end, since the "relationship" never really began. Raising your awareness in this way will empower you to move on when it is time.

You do not have time for email banter. Be in today. It's all we have. As Kahlil Gibran described children in *The Prophet*: "Their souls dwell in the house of tomorrow, which you cannot visit, not even in your dreams."

B. Texting and Tribulation

Texting is distracting. You're missing out on the beauty swirling around you. The Golden State Warriors could walk by and you wouldn't notice. Dogs could be wagging you warm greetings, and then gazing sadly after you as you walked away without petting them. You could miss out on your grandchildren's lives if you ignore them in favor of Android power. If you text, text quickly and then reenter Now. And remember: the last person to text in an exchange loses.

Excessive text messages hound and enslave both recipient and sender, distracting from the moment. As with an abused substance, more and more are required until addiction debilitates and disables.

Texting is for brief factual information—i.e., questions such as the following:

1. Where are you?
2. What time will you be here?

The fact that we constantly have to ask, "Where are you?" proves that we no longer see people, talk to them or know them, much less know their whereabouts. In the time before cell phones, we weren't compelled to inquire about people's whereabouts because 1) we didn't give a damn; 2) our relationships were based upon trust so we didn't feel compelled constantly to stalk our mates; and 3) we were smart enough to know that constantly pestering our partner would eventually get on his last nerve. Give your fellow earthlings (and yourself) some breathing room!

There is, however, an advantage to texting—it helps you stay young. You can enjoy perfecting the art, although not behind the wheel or while operating heavy machinery. Texting requires conciseness, thus exercising the brain.

C. When to Have a Real Phone Conversation

A discussion of "upping the ante" can only begin after your screening process has filtered out Excessive Emailer, Cyberbully and Man-Up Man. In short, you must already have weeded out the predators from the potentials. Real men don't fear the phone. They don't hide. Their in-your-face confidence is not dependent upon carefully tailored self-descriptions in overthought emails; they decide and act in real time.

1. Excessive Emailer

A "Master of the Universe" will rarely initiate a telephone dialog; he can't stand surprises, and he fears an evenly balanced playing field where he must think on his feet. In fact, he will rarely if ever initiate anything, including relationships. Fueled by the false confidence that the internet's anonymity inspires, he incorrectly believes that he has truth, justice, and the American Way on his side. But fear paralyzes him each time he picks up the phone. His voicemail recording instructs to leave a "detailed" message because he needs to meticulously prepare which particular bullying strategy he will employ during his next email. Even then, summoning the balls to pick up the phone is overwhelming for him. He is an over-analyzer, not a doer, and spends hours constructing overly organized emails that no reasonable person would ever bother to answer. He will use your lack of response as justification for yet another "follow-up" email. His two favorite phrases, "follow-up" and "What is the status of …" are indeed red flags in and of themselves. And he will send confirmation emails when prior communications have left *no doubt* as to the terms of an agreement or understanding. Confirming a date is a bad sign—it shows lack of confidence. A cowboy doesn't phone ahead for pizza and then call to confirm the order. He walks in and the waitress brings him the usual. It ain't that hard.

2. Cyberbully

Cyberbullying is emailing on steroids. Only while basking in his monitor's comforting glare can Cyberbully be truly brave. Only here can he have the last word and sustain the illusion of control. Cyberbully's greatest joy is sending a derisive, dismissive email. Such whiners are also predators. They can survive only in professions in which the cards are stacked in their favor, because they are incapable of winning evenly matched races. On a true battlefield, unbuttressed by a built-in advantage, Cyberbully quickly expires. He gravitates toward the "powerful" professions, mistakenly believing he personally controls that power, much like librarians believe they own the books they shelve and stamp so diligently. True power emanates gently but firmly from within. Not from superficial status and trappings of a profession which cloak the "professional" in a magic cape.

3. Man–Up Man

After screening out Excessive Emailer and Cyberbully, Man-Up Man will be easy to spot. Man-Up Man drags it out too long. You'll know when the emails and texts are no longer enough. Electric shadows will not stroke your forehead as you lie dying, when you most need to be loved. Imagine Man-Up Man as your health care power of attorney, sending your ICU doctor a text message to pull the plug. Man-Up Man lives via text.

The creation of a relationship, just as its disintegration, has stages. Although the phases of grief don't always manifest themselves at predictable times or in a foreseeable order, each makes its cameo. The creation of new relationships is the same. It may take time and some trial and error. But when you're dealing with a card-carrying "Man-Up Man," his constant need for second, third, and fiftieth chances will merely lengthen your misery, uncertainty, and false hope. You don't have time to enable a man like that. Know your time limit and stick to it.

If he misses his chance, it's not your responsibility to explain to him what he did wrong. You are interviewing him for a job. Prospective employers look for three things: 1) Does he want the job? 2) Can he do the job? and 3) Is he manageable? He who fails to man up at the appropriate time fails on all counts. He isn't motivated to be on your team or to love you. If Man-Up has never passed beyond the email stage, you can't fully assess his sense of humor or his sincerity, because you are unable to observe his body language. If you don't meet him in person you may never see the kindness in his eyes, or the violence. Let him go.

IX

Your Family and His Family

A. His Two-Legger Relatives

Assess early on his openness to people from diverse cultural backgrounds. Does he deny or embrace his unique lineage? If the former, he may be a self-hater. If the latter, he'll probably be open-minded with you as well, respect your differences of opinion and occasionally be comfortable with an agreement to disagree instead of badgering you to parrot his every view. Does he have family connections? Whether someone lives alone in a dark basement is not usually apparent from a dating site profile. But beware the signs. Too many family pictures may veil the truth. Too many pics from formal events such as weddings or holiday parties, when social norm compels togetherness, may signal underlying dysfunction. Look for pictures of people at spontaneous gatherings, people whose affection and respect for each other are boldly apparent. You'll know it when you see it.

You may need to decide how you feel about taking care of his children and grandchildren. You may think that if you have no grandchildren that this will be a great opportunity for you to be a grandmother. Don't assume it will be so easy. You will never replace the grandmother whose time with them was cut short through death, divorce or disaster. But you can work your way into their hearts, just as you establish any other relationship: by earning trust, being reliable and loving unconditionally.

Give your man some space, and time to spend alone with his family uninterrupted by your interference and directives. You don't have to be part of all conversations in all forums, and you and Prospect are not joined at the hip. Remain silent, back off, and let them love without you. There are things you can never share. You'll give yourself some sorely needed alone time in the process. You don't always have to spend holidays together. Prospect and his family need to reminisce about the days before You. Keep your own soul mate's memory in a place in your heart where you alone can visit. Those times—comic and tragic—are part of you; don't let them be silenced by memories of bad news imparted by divorce lawyers or the callous doctors who barred you from your soul mate's room during intubation. These recent memories are powerful and insidious. Weave the positive memories into a new tapestry—your wedding day, your children's births, funny moments, thoughtful gifts and gestures. Expect some setbacks until you master the art; time and patience encourage the process.

Pay close attention to how he treats his mother. This tells you more about who he is, and how he will treat you, than anything else. Does he call her just to chat every few days? Does he send her birthday cards and flowers, a Valentine and Godiva chocolate? A big Christmas stocking? This tells you what he thinks of her, and of himself. Or does he just whine and complain about some real or imagined wrong that she committed against him as a toddler? Of course, if he suffered a legitimate wrong such as abuse, you need to listen and help him address it. But if he's whining about never having received a pony or some other childhood luxury, then be kind and listen but recognize a Man-Up Man when you see one and respond accordingly.

B. Your Two-Legger Relatives

Your family got you through this disaster; be there for them, just as you encourage him to be there for his family. Any prospect who does not accept this is not for you. Don't become the "prize" in a competition between Prospect and your family. Don't encourage, reinforce, or acquiesce to such contests. There is enough time and love for everyone.

C. Beloved Four-Leggers

If you and Prospect each bring a dog into the relationship and you each sleep with your respective four-legger, care must be exercised to ensure that all humans and dogs get what they need. With planning and sometimes even professional help, the planets can realign into a calming and pleasant orbit. The dogs' humans must both be committed to as smooth a transition as possible, to making it work even if there are rough spots along the way. The key here, when merging families or fish or pet iguanas, is to take it slow and easy. You can't make your kids like other kids. And you can't make your dogs like other dogs. They may eventually learn to peacefully coexist. If you and/or your new partner sleeps with a dog, forgoing that may be upsetting for both dog and owner. But the dog may be able to learn to sleep in a bed nearby, even a dog-sized bunk bed set up next to yours so he can stare soulfully at you in the morning. Only you know whether the person you think you may have finally found is worth this adjustment for you and your pet. Think it through. You are the world to your dog. All she's got. Make it work, with professional help if necessary.

X

Widening the Circle

A. His Friends: You Might Not Like Them but Can You Deal with Them?

Friendships take time and effort. Most people have friends, but if Prospect has recently faced the financial and/or emotional poverty of divorce or widowerhood, he simply may not have been able to sustain healthy relationships. If he does have friends, show them respect but don't be their doormat. Don't let him invite them over to smoke cigars and leave potato chip grease stains in the living room you slaved on Saturday morning to vacuum. If he throws the party, he vacuums. If he's retired and you're working, then he does all vacuuming, no matter whose party it was.

If he's too close to one friend, and that friend is dirtying up your sofa a little too often, remind Prospect that you live here and Moochman does not. Real men don't spend the night with other men. You don't want to have to bother putting on a bra every time you step out of your bedroom and into what Moochman's omnipresence has transformed into the "common area" of your two-bedroom.

Prospect may have holdover couple friends from his previous relationship. Probably not a good idea for you to continue as the newly substituted member. You won't be accepted. If you want to chance it once just to show him it won't work, go ahead, but proceed with caution. The same holds true with your own couple friends from yesteryear. They were probably as fond or fonder of your ex as of you and will resent Prospect. And he will feel like an outsider as he's regaled with stories of adventures enjoyed by the four of you before he was even born.

For the newly widowed, try going out to dinner once with one of your old couple friends. Now is the time to face that empty chair. It's part of the process; get it over with. You won't be invited again. They only wanted to help, didn't realize it would be this awkward. Avoid them from here on out but give them credit for trying.

Don't try too hard to impress his friends, and don't sweat it if not all of them like you. Just relax and be yourself. Try, but not desperately. Smile and listen. Acknowledge the power they hold over Prospect, and the power they potentially hold, therefore, over you. If the bullet meets the bone, they may become your best supporters. When Prospect asks for their advice about you, it won't hurt for them to have your back. His friends may feel twangs of grief as he pulls away from them and toward you, particularly if his new relationship means an end to their Friday night barhopping. His friends may, like certain of his family members, try to compete with you for him. Get the "nights out with the guys" as well as the "girls' nights out" resolved as best you can before embarking upon monogamy. If you and Prospect move in together, he won't have much time for them. Recognition of this fact may drive Prospect into his Man Cave for a while—cigars and all—or off on a hunting trip involving firearms. Every man fears loss of control, and a fish fights hardest right before it flops. If Prospect's unemployed friends goad him into staying out late and coming home drunk, lay down the law as soon as he's sobered up, and take no prisoners. The unemployed can sleep it off the next day; Prospect can't. He needs to be well rested in order to fulfill his duties to you and to society. He needs to remain alcohol-free, since he will need every last one of his sorry brain cells to engage in the many arguments you will instigate for your own entertainment. But stay on your toes. Prospect learns fast, and remember, he is learning from the best.

Another downside of friends who don't work is that Prospect will be paying their drinking tabs. The unemployed are sometimes quite entertaining, people you wouldn't mind sitting down at a bar with (if you were a drinking woman). Or perhaps starving artists who can stay up into the wee hours discussing Nietzsche, outsider art and backward causality. The later it gets, the more interesting they become. But you're in your sixties now and it's just real hard to stay up for those wee-hour powwows, decaf your only fuel.

A word about his friends on the force. Cops understand the seamier side of life and are trained to communicate with people from all socioeconomic levels. But deep down, although many are on a noble mission, some are driven by the need for power and control over others and are therefore unable to invest in the give and take that a relationship needs to survive. But if your man's hanging out with fellow law enforcement, you can rest assured they will do their best to protect those around them and each other. As friendships go, your man could do a whole lot worse.

Now to his office "colleagues." He will have opportunities: long lunches and business trips involving alcohol and late nights. His success will make him attractive to many who are interested only in his money or the favors he can bestow. So, if your radar detects infidelity, keep in mind that you might have to reenter the dating pool if this guy flies the coop. But if he is loyal and a keeper don't start developing a Plan B that could distract you from your Plan A. Be in the moment.

There is little you can do to discourage his potential desire to stray, other than monitoring without smothering him. If you try to tie him to your hip he will flee, and rightly so. Nobody wants a clinger. But show him who's boss. This can be accomplished with meatloaf and potatoes. It's quite simple. Few real men can resist the inviting comfort of a warm kitchen, a beer, and a TV remote. If you want true commitment, mash the potatoes and add gravy. If he's temporarily distracted by the female colleague who lets him treat her to frozen "Cosmopolitans" after work, the call of three squares will soon drown out the pink drink's siren song. No contest.

If he does stray with a female friend, then let him own up to it. If he confesses and demonstrates true remorse through his actions, consider giving him another chance. But if he takes that second chance you give him, don't be bitter about it and make him pay forever. And keep a squeaky-clean slate yourself. But if your slate gathers some chalk now and again, forgive yourself for it. Feeling guilty forever about an occasional harmless fantasy or an indiscretion on your part can interfere with your karma and newfound positivity. It can also be more damaging to your relationship than hashing it out with your man. If he is understanding and reasonable, and you believe he will forgive you, and if you love him and want to maintain your relationship with him, discuss it with him and come prepared to do your part in fixing whatever led to the slip. If he won't go to counseling, then go yourself. Except in cases in which you are experiencing mental or physical abuse, you may be as much a part of the problem as he. Risks accompany disclosure by him or by you, but relationships are fraught with risks—and rewards.

B. Your Friends: He Might Not Like Them—Or He Might Like Them Too Much!

Always be clear with your friends that you value their honesty. If Prospect hits on them you want to know. That's Prospect's fault, not your friends'. Encourage your friends to report all of his emotional and spiritual violations, not just physical indiscretions. Train your friends to be good little soldiers and wellsprings of information, both positive and negative. Be clear with them that you want no sugar coating—the clock's ticking, and there's no time left for flimsy gingerbread houses that crumble in the wind, inviting though they may appear. The flower of youth is fading and you have no time to slow dance with fantasy.

What if Prospect tells you that your friend hit on *him*? He's lying. No man would claim this except as a ruse to hide the fact that he hit on your friend. Adios.

XI

How to Sustain a Relationship

A. Is It Worth Sustaining—Is He the One?

Before investing time in sustaining a relationship, assess it. Prepare a simple chart. List his pros in the left-hand column, his cons on the right. Is he reliable? Does he go on benders? Get into arguments with your family about politics, delight in criticizing your parents, friends or your personal physical qualities? Like a progressive disease, these negative characteristics will feed upon themselves, gradually morphing into an enemy more formidable than MRSA.

Test him. Does he have more than one phone? There is rarely a legitimate reason for an individual to possess more than one cell phone (unless one phone is devoted exclusively to a bona fide business). Ask him these and other questions, then face the answers. When did he last check in on the dating sites? Twenty minutes ago? Information about when a user was last on a site, or how long he or she has been active on a site, is sometimes available on the site or app. However, the accuracy of such information is reliable only if properly updated. Of course, if you use your real profile he may figure out you have been searching. So, if you want to play hard-to-get, or you don't want to encourage him before you have sufficient information, then this is perhaps not the best tactic. On the other hand, is there really a downside to him knowing that you may be interested? You can't afford to lose track of time in unending dalliances, but a certain degree of relationship building banter is an integral part of The Chase.

Sustaining a relationship in which one partner is employed and the other retired is next to impossible. "'Til Death Do Us Part" requires both parties to be available for in-person joint activities. This doesn't have to mean elaborate trips on world cruises. Just watching TV and eating popcorn with real butter can get you there. And get two bowls. He needs to run his own popcorn program and stay out of yours.

If he's retired he may promote two-week trips in his RV to the Wild West. You don't want to be dragged to overscheduled events and ridiculous rafting trips. So, if he is retired and you're not, encourage him to join a club or to do some volunteer work. Otherwise he'll be camped out at the computer all day trolling the internet trying to figure out how to use the 200,000 frequent flier miles he has to use or lose by next week. But if you are too unavailable for his antics, he will grow to resent his solitude and rejoin dating sites to combat his own boredom and to get even with you for ignoring him. Sometimes—and you'll know when those times are—throw him a bone.

B. Long-Distance Longing

Online relationships, without more, are dead ends. If Prospect lives far away, you will need a lot of money for plane fare, and time to travel.

If you're lucky, your parents and siblings are still with you. They have probably put you first more times than you can count and way more often than you deserved. So, if you are privileged to have them close by and the health to help them when they need it, put them first. Any relocation decision must be voted down unless you can fulfill your responsibility to your parents, aunts, uncles, and siblings. Any worthy Prospect will understand this and will be equally committed to his own family.

Uprooting is hard—you may have been through it recently after your divorce or your soul mate's death. Your stuff has to be sorted, reflected upon and in some cases relinquished. Each stick of furniture, each book, each Christmas ornament, has a memory. Sometimes it's just easier to stay in the marital home with your memories, at least for a while. But the presence of his shadows and looking over at the reclining chair where he sat, can be even more painful than the first time you saw him in his casket or held the urn. You were able to brace yourself for that, you steeled yourself, you were ready. But the empty chair subtly creeps into your peripheral vision when you least expect it.

Get rid of the clutter breeding around you. Transform items on the edge of your consciousness into positive messages that delight and inspire. Ditch that old battered quilted purse that screams "dowdy." And get comfortable yourself in your soul mate's recliner. Shifting around your stuff will make moving easier.

C. W-O-R-K

Some sixty-year-olds conclude they can be themselves, and if people don't like them for who they are, then tough. Don't fall into that trap. Just because you're sixty doesn't mean your relationships will require any less effort than they did at twenty-five. In fact, they require more because the competition is stiffer. And you may have less energy now than you did at that age to play the games that are a necessary part of the process, or to apply mascara or body glitter.

So, when you're deciding whether the relationship is worth sustaining, remember that it's going to require real work. Do not leave all social planning to Prospect. Suggest, do not demand. Don't drag him kicking and screaming to boring symphony performances or plays. Rent *Fury Road* and watch it together. You'll have him then, particularly if meatloaf is involved.

Don't shepherd him to flea markets. Flea markets probably aren't doing you any good either, because chances are you already have too much stuff. Donate your current crap; someone can use that pink boa that was part of your Halloween costume ten years ago. Let it become someone else's crap. If you are attached to a Halloween costume or some other knick-knack, take a photo before you donate it.

Let him take you to a haunted house where you can be chased by a ghoul with a fake chainsaw. Hold Prospect's hand and look to him for protection as you stagger through the fake fog. A haunted house mirrors life: twists and turns, scary creatures popping out at you, the hall of mirrors and bad-ass clowns with creepy smiles. Prospect will protect you and love you more for letting him be a real man.

Figure out what you can do for him. If he's a Three Stooges fan, buy him an e-book about them or subscribe to a service from which he can access their movies. Show that you've been thinking about him. Get him a bobblehead of his favorite rock star or athlete. Tailor part of your world to his but keep your own world and your own past alive in your heart and close by, for reference and inner strength.

Find out his favorite foods, colors, and music. But don't press for too many details. You don't have to spend a lot of money to cook a good meal, and biscuits seal the deal. Does he genuinely appreciate your efforts? Sharing a meal that you've cooked for him will reveal whether he's a finicky whiner. Does he whine because the gravy is too thick? The slaw not creamy enough? No matter how bad the spaghetti is, his praise needs to be unconditional. However, always find out if he has any dietary restrictions before you cook for him. If you sense that he's not ready to share this, cooking may not be a good idea just yet.

Listen to him. It would be unmanly of him to let you solve his problems, so don't try. Lend him your ear. If you truly listen, the ideas that spew forth from the nether regions of his man-brain will grow and improve exponentially.

Be proud of him. Tell his family that you are. But more important, tell him that you are. And tell him why.

Don't try to get revenge on him for an affair he had when he was married to his former wife back in the Sixties. The statute of limitations on that offense has long since run. Arguments shouldn't be about winning, but about fixing something that's broken and about moving forward. And what's usually broken is the way that you communicate with each other. Find someone who can truly listen to you when you're angry (which is a lot easier to do when you're not hurling insults). And listen to him when he's angry. Is he trying to make things better? Or does he just want to hurt your feelings to extract revenge for some real or imagined wrong? If it's the latter, dump him.

He will usually need the remote—and just when you're involved in a riveting melodrama or fashion show. Sitting through an ever-changing array of shoot-'em-up car chases while he frantically channel surfs might be annoying, but it might be preferable to watching alone. Work at making some concessions.

D. Stages of Connection

You're old and you're going to get older. Decide what you want, and who or what will fulfill your needs. Surround yourself with people who make you happy and to whom you matter. Develop and maintain your relationships in ways that are right for you. You may not need constant excitement, monogamy, cohabitation or marriage—in fact, now that time is running out it's even more important that you choose the level of involvement that makes you the happiest. Then embrace your choice—no need to apologize for or explain it. Revisit your decision when the time is right.

1. Just a Pen Pal

Email correspondence may be the first step in sustaining a relationship, but daily emails without face-to-face meetings, phone calls, or Skype, cannot take a relationship to the next level. New Digital Man can be your rebound, but if he can't move it forward, end it. However much it hurts, your friends are unlikely to understand what you're going through since they didn't know him. But let them try to help.

A pen pal relationship has its place, however, and can be an end unto itself. Positive human contact, such as emails that evoke laughter, happiness and compassion, exercise the brain and momentarily eradicate painful memories. Such relationships can distract and entertain so long as they are recognized for what they are—light and friendly flirtations without strings or 3-D shoulders to cry on.

2. Companion

Deep down where it matters, we all want someone to laugh with. Dating sites try to introduce people who at least profess similar interests. Shared movie, reading, and exercise preferences can engender compatibility. Do you really want to be dragged to horror flicks that will give you bad dreams for six months and cause you to need antipsychotics? Can you sit through ten more tiresome car chases as your chronic motion sickness kicks in? On the other hand, try not to rule out entire movie genres. Some horror films are so scary they're funny, and some car chases amusing in their preposterousness. Gear as much of your life as possible to what makes you laugh.

The most important factor in companionability is a shared sense of humor. Does he get why you think a certain premise is flawed to the point of hilarity? Do you laugh when he tells you that because it's Valentine's Day you can check out any book you want from the public library? Because your time is now more valuable than ever, humor and positivity are more important than ever.

3. Partner

Marrying a certain type of person does not guarantee reliability, particularly if your partner drinks too much or otherwise rationalizes his absence at events of importance to you, i.e., by claiming he doesn't like crowds. This comes as no surprise to you, because your recent loss has taught you that there are no guarantees in the Valley of the Shadow of Death. But if you're looking for stability, your best bet is "Partner."

A critical component in all business partnerships is the sharing of profits and losses. Same holds true in social partnerships. Some days you might get stuck tailgating, but on other days Partner will kindly sit through a movie you chose. If you want a partner, seek reliability, stability and financial security, and develop a high tolerance for boredom. If Partner says he'll be somewhere at 5:30, he'll probably be early (and hoppin' mad if you are late).

4. Lover Wannabes

a. The Self-Professed "Romantic." No true lover describes himself as "romantic." If Señor Romatique were really romantic, he'd still be married. This self-description is designed to convey that although his first marriage did not work out he has learned his lesson and is ready to buy roses. Don't fall for this. He's either fooling himself or trying to fool you.

b. The Self-Professed Thrill Seeker. When someone says he is "looking for someone who is willing to try new things," he is conveying that he wants a sexually innovative partner who will do what HE wants when HE wants it. He's definitely taking medication for erectile dysfunction and wants someone who can keep up with him, or better put, with him on Viagra. Steer clear, this one's a self-centered no-win.

c. The Self-Professed Wealthy and/or "Sensitive Guy." Weed out the self-promoters and anyone who lists their income as 300K+. With rare exceptions, and I know one, the richer the man, the bigger the bully. And beware of the self-described "sensitive guy." If true, which it probably is not, it means he can't take a joke. You have no time to tiptoe around fragile egos.

d. The Self-Professed "Hunk." Here we have the body builder or real athlete who puts his hands behind his head when talking to you, armpit stains optional. Facial features distorted by excessive steroid use. He probably eats weird things and may criticize you for not following his dietary regimen du jour. (He refuses to discuss the fact that his previous regimen was correlated in recent FDA studies with significant health risks.)

Athletes can be great, and you want someone who takes care of himself in any event. But you don't want someone who's more in love with his muscle-bound body than he'll ever be with you. The same discipline that drives him daily to the gym may drive him to apply unreasonable and unnecessary standards to you.

5. The True Lover: Carpe Diem

They're out there. In grocery stores. Looking for Grand Marnier and green cards. Just seeing them standing there evokes the Sixties' freedom, craziness, and happy times. Beatniks in coffee shops espousing anarchy. We loved the show. The Lover attempting to draw fellow hippies on the campus quadrangle under his spell. The female passersby reeking of patchouli oil and smiling, quietly worshiping Lover, hoping to be next summoned. Entranced by his mystery and by the revolution.

"Socrates" was his name. He had a following twice as big and twice as emotional as a Greek chorus. His invitations to all-night parties had been run off in two colors on a mimeograph machine of old. No one ever knew his major, or his last name. A gleaming yet elusive star in the foreign party scene. Lover is powerful, as unattainable now as then. You fear him, yet fear drives you to him. So, you pursue him after you reject him, but by then it is too late.

Lover drinks whisky straight up. No monkeying around with olives or umbrellas. Ice is a frivolity best consigned to garden party punchbowls. Lover may drink a fine wine, but he knows enough to speak of it only by comparing its properties to yours.

The one who got away? You might reconsider if your Google search results in a link to "Free Socrates" …

6. Going It Alone

Don't beat yourself up if you don't really need a lover, husband, or confidante. Some people are fiercely independent and excel alone. But being an island can be rough. Paying all your own bills, answering your own questions, solving your own problems. When you take your car in to be fixed, you have to wait for it and debate with the mechanic predators. You have to put air into your tires and be sure the vehicle maintenance schedule gets stamped at each visit. This is not difficult, just extremely tedious. Ask your friends for help with certain tasks, but don't take advantage of them. Save favors for when you really need them. And most of all, be there for your family and friends in their times of need.

You, the newly single, have no one to review your to-do list with. So, master it yourself. Don't make a big deal about it or you'll spend half a day making lists and never start anything. Pick a day, pick a time, sit down. Do it for fun, do it because you love being organized, but most of all, do it to focus your future. Being alone requires discipline—you have no one other than yourself to tell you to get back to work.

Being alone doesn't mean being lonely. Solitude can rejuvenate. There's nothing wrong with relishing the recliner at the end of the day. If you have a job that requires you to deal with bullies you can't stand, those moments of relaxation will be the fuel you'll need to fight back. "This game hasn't even started yet," as my soul mate used to say when there were only two minutes left in a Chicago Bulls game.

Guard your privacy. Don't get sucked into ongoing social arrangements that can overwhelm and suffocate, well-intentioned though the group may be. These events are rarely good forums for meeting potential soul mates, as you tend to simply rehash the same old issues with the same old people. But they may have much to offer outside the realm of your search for a Prospect. Individuals within the group may be godsends and trustworthy confidantes, particularly if they can boost your confidence and make you laugh. Just manage your expectations and resist any inflexible routine that prevents you from being you.

Whether you choose to meet the future alone or with a partner, use your remaining years to transform yourself totally. As you move forward, keep your options open by truly experiencing Now. You're sure to find surprises if you pry yourself off the phone long enough. A tattooed hard-body, jeans slightly tattered, one wrist adorned with simple thin leather and silver bands, stands leaning against a battered brick wall in a Paris alley, in partial shadow. His glance acknowledges you in a way you thought no longer possible, causing you to forget past and future for the first time since Soul Mate's death. Unless you act, you may never see him again. Recognizing that action is an option is a step forward even if you choose not to act. And if that is your choice, the Future will come soon enough, spreading her legs like a willing mistress.

XII

How to Turn Dating into Marriage— Or Decide Not to Bother

A. How to Turn the Tide toward Marriage If He Is the One

You will know quickly when you have found him. Ask yourself one thing—can you rely on this two-legger to take you to the ER in the middle of the night without bitching you out? To console you when you're sad? To speak logically with you when you need analysis? Is he willing to stop what he is doing and focus on you? Does he love you enough to make the right decision if he were asked by the doctor whether to pull the plug? Reliability is romantic. Only the reliable male can truly rescue you. The flimflam vegan won't be there for the rough times; he'll be out eating tofu on your nickel.

The ICU forces soul bearing. Final professions of love, final confessions, and love's superseding of those wrongs. You've been through this once; you know how it ends. Pick the person you want to escort you to the door, humanely, and with compassion and love.

Maybe your soul mate's death was sudden and you did not have the luxury of a final good-bye or confession. Such an experience underscores the need to find a significant other this time around with whom you can communicate the important stuff on a daily basis. This way, if you were later to be deprived of a final good-bye, you would already have told each other what really mattered and would have no regrets.

Does he stand by you in a crunch, or does he disrespect you by interrupting your most vulnerable thoughts that took some courage for you to share with him in the first place? Does he belittle you in front of others, challenge you constantly, and argue incessantly about meaningless details? Or does he just go with it if it's right, regardless of who came up with the idea? Does he show up late for events or appointments that are important to you? What time we have left should not be spent waiting for some spoiled brat to finally show up hung over in a ratty T-shirt.

Evaluate his clothing and accessories as part of your preliminary screening. Real Man does not use a beach towel, but just grabs any old beige-ass bath towel that he scrounges up. Whatever is most convenient for him. No turquoise sea turtles or conch shell motifs mirroring the pattern on his speedo. Brand names are irrelevant to Real Man.

And pick the person you would be honored to help through life's occasional "Sturm und Drang"—conflicts with his family; health, financial, and personal crises. Pick someone you respect.

So, you've surmounted all of these hurdles. You've weaned out the predators, the egomaniacs, the moochers and whiners. You've found him. The One.

If you're not fooling yourself, he will find a way to be with you, miles and heartaches and past baggage aside. Even though you have decided he's worth it, let him prove his worth by standing tall in your eyes and pursuing you. It's not about *playing* hard to get—you really *are* hard to get. He needs to be schooled on this issue early on so that he will learn your value. Don't ditch your friends and family just to tag along after him. If he falls through, you'll berate yourself for throwing your friends and family under the bus. Don't fail them. They were there before you met your soul mate, they listened to you when you lost him, and they'll be there, if you're lucky, long after any prospect who doesn't pass your tests. Treasure them.

Don't text him 25 times a day. Absent emergency, one or two texts per day are usually sufficient. If Prospect thinks he has to be texted more than once a day or has to know your every move via text update, he is too needy and insecure.

He has the burden of proof. Let him work his way into your schedule and your heart. He must continue to win you over if life is to remain interesting. If he is a real man, this will come naturally. If he is not a real man, he will become predictable, complacent, boring and sedentary.

When do you raise the subject of exclusivity? Don't give him an ultimatum. Give yourself one. Be willing to walk away. A wordless moment enjoying a sunset or a rain can inspire a mutual vision of you as a couple. Exclusivity is sensed, but not necessarily discussed.

B. How to End It with Minimal Pain If He Isn't the One

Even if both of you want it to be over, neither of you may want to be the bad guy. Take charge of the end, regardless of whether it's your idea. Taking control over this will ease your fear of loneliness. Don't stand in one place while he walks away. Be gone when he leaves. Even if this only means being out of the house when he drives away in his debt-saddled male midlife crisis car. And no matter how many times his overwhelming guilt drives him to text you after the breakup, don't text back. It's over. You have no time for bad emotional investments in freefall.

If the end was your idea, be compassionate if circumstances warrant. No need to increase his grief any more than the end will do on its own. Once your decision is final, don't backslide into the relationship. Don't allow him to reenter your world unless you are both serious about starting over. As with concerns surrounding the "right to die," such encounters may not prolong the relationship, but rather, its end.

If he ended it, eventually you will forgive him and thank him for his lack of responsibility and for the childish decisions of late onset male menopause, because this means you're rid of him. It's like cutting off an arm before the gangrene spreads. Sure, you'll miss him for a while, but your survival is not dependent upon him. No loss could ever rival the loss you have just survived. And no other personal victory could ever trump that survival.

Your emotions after Fly-by-Night's exit are inconsequential next to the tsunami of your soul mate's death. A primary advantage of being suddenly single at sixty is that most losses are virtually inconsequential compared to the Big Bang you've just endured. Express these emotions to a trusted friend or counselor. And find a counselor who can shorten your to-do list and help you prioritize it, a counselor who has a heart of gold and yet holds you accountable.

XIII

Chemistry—the Holy Grail or a Mirage?

Open virtually any women's magazine and you will find numerous articles about chemistry, articles that debate and microanalyze its dynamics and promote various products to enhance it. The concept is no different at sixty than it was at twenty—people either are or are not physically attracted to each other.

At sixty, we may be tempted to place less importance on how attractive others are to us, because there are fewer men to choose from and we just cannot be as picky as we used to be. Some sixty-year-olds persist in the athletic routines of their youth, usually because they are just too bullheaded to change old habits. They unwisely refuse to acknowledge their mortality, and in so failing, risk what life they have left by embracing irregular and unadvisable exercise routines. Be in the moment during exercise and listen to your body's signals. Physical fitness can be a positive force in the chemistry equation.

Don't be afraid to create chemistry by flaunting your own attractiveness. You don't have to "dress your age." Go to the junior department of any major store and you will find treasure troves of items that are "age-appropriate," if you absolutely must use that phrase. Long, fitted sweaters that cover the derriere, for instance. You don't have to wear the loose-fitting, elastic-waist pants with matching blazers sold as "separates." (Even that word is depressing, like they're assuming you have a huge ass and a small top and you have to shop there to get something that fits both body parts.) Cut a wide berth around the separates department, and head instead for "Young Professionals" or "Juniors." You may have worn black to the funeral, but now is the time to think color and confidence. Powerful colors that will help you turn and walk away when you need to. Well placed, tasteful bold colors that flaunt your fearlessness—red, gold and chartreuse in tasteful moderation.

Shopping can be streamlined and affordable if correctly planned—know what day the truck arrives at your favorite retail outlets and ask if they have senior discount days (many do). Be assertive in asking for discounts for slightly damaged goods which "no one will notice from a trotting horse" as my great grandmother used to say. Gently antiqued garments are all the rage these days, but you may want to rethink the torn jean look since they risk exposure of that varicose vein you've been meaning to talk to your doctor about.

Loosen your definition of chemistry—let it be a moment, not an eternity. Don't demand that it single-handedly drive the relationship 100% or even 50% of the time. If you can find some dude attractive even for a nanosecond during the day, call it chemistry. If you can see him pondering a weighty issue or work of art and are favorably impressed by his intellect and vision, broaden the concept of chemistry to include that fleeting feeling. We're not saying he deserves it, but you do. Open up the definition and the moment. If he opens a jar for you or hangs a picture or changes a tire or a light bulb, let that be a chemistry moment. Chemistry can retain its reputation as the holy grail of relationships, but only if you keep its definition fluid. It may be a mirage that evaporates as you approach it. But if you believe in that moment, that fleeting sensation of chemistry will not disappoint.

XIV

The Five Circles of Life

A. Spiritual

Spiritual life—connecting to and being guided by a higher power—plays a huge role in the healing process. Each person's spiritual reality is unique. Some commune daily with a higher power alone, others at a mosque or church. Spiritual leaders are among us—ministers, imams, rabbis, priests, televangelists, politicians, life coaches, counselors, colleagues, friends and muses. Be open to their sometimes subtle presence. God will be happy to hear from you. As children of yon Sixties many of us did not embrace organized religion back then. But at sixty we have learned to listen and soul search. So, don't be shackled by any past prejudice against the concept of a higher power. Let your life be guided by what drives you now.

Allow yourself to be inspired by art—weaving, sculpture, pottery, music—something you loved in the past but have not had time to pursue until now. Art that is about pain can also help you understand and share your own pain, so that you can release it. Opening your mind in this way and becoming part of something bigger than you gives you the tools to reach more deeply into calm, reflective moments of inspiration and understanding, and to connect you with what matters.

The spiritual world speaks if we listen. Sometimes it speaks faintly or indirectly, but always profoundly. A sudden thought or memory that we shared with someone no longer with us. Or when answers come or problems seem to solve themselves as we lie in bed shortly after awakening.

B. Physical

Assume responsibility for your physical well-being—diet, exercise, attractiveness to others. Holding yourself accountable for these things, and setting realistic goals, will increase self-esteem and success. Stop making excuses. You have gained weight not because you are "big boned" or "retaining water." Absent rare medical circumstances, your weight gain can be explained by a sedentary lifestyle and too many calories. Or by too much rich but comforting funeral food. Stress is a good excuse for overeating. Medicate yourself with food if you must, but only as a short-term coping mechanism. Then it's over and time to step up to the plate—with less food on it.

When improving your physical self, deal with only one problem at a time. If you need to stop smoking, do it and quit talking about it. Your family wants you around for a long time. You don't need medication or group therapy to quit smoking. Just wean yourself off gradually, down to one a day, and then one every other day and eventually you will forget to smoke. But don't try to diet and quit smoking at the same time. You risk crashing and burning on both counts. And if you want to quit drinking, tackle that separately. You'll feel too sorry for yourself to hold yourself accountable if you try to go cold turkey on everything at once, unless of course your doctor has advised it and you have no legitimate reason to doubt his or her medical opinion.

As with spiritual tutors, there are an abundance of physical tutors—physical therapists, personal trainers, weight-loss gurus, Pilates and salsa instructors, and your friends. By keeping in physical shape, you will be more in tune with the other primary aspects of your life.

C. Family

The inner circle of your family must be cultivated and preserved. Do not limit your family to those related to you by blood or marriage. Embrace your children's friends, who see you through your children's eyes. If you were to ever lose a child, these friends would share that child's memory with you. At sixty you see the value of this, something that would not have occurred to you before, back when you thought you and Soul Mate were bulletproof.

Welcome deserving members of the animal kingdom into the inner circle of your family and your heart. They are loyal and forgiving. And there are no better judges of character. If your cat relieves himself in a beanbag chair Prospect has just sat in, heed the warning. Let your dog bark at people who come to your door. That's his job, and it's yours to take notice. Dogs are the most wondrous teachers of human values—kindness, loyalty, self-confidence, happiness and forgiveness. Their warmth, love and devotion can trigger the calm merging of your spiritual and family spheres. They will bring you otherworldly joy, and when they go will tear it from you. But you will survive that, too—you have a track record now. If you lose a loyal four-legged friend, you might be comforted by "Rainbow Bridge," a beautiful poem about pets' afterlives.[5]

D. Friends

Friendships, like houses, require maintenance. Don't always rely on the other person to initiate social events. At first, it's best not to plan too much in advance—what with having to solve all your own problems and all, you may find it difficult to work any type of social life into the convoluted network of your grieving process.

Here are some tips:

1.) Make no plans with women who begin an invitation with, "Oh, Mike's out of town—wanna do a Girls' Night Out on Thursday?" Of course the spouse comes first, but emphasizing this fact in such a crass manner is grossly insensitive, and makes your newfound loneliness even lonelier. Sometimes, you simply must set these insensitive people straight. They don't know how they sound or they would be shutting up much more frequently. They sometimes see life only through their own myopic perspectives. So, when presented with such a left-handed invitation, say, "You know, Suzi, your suggestion makes me feel like I'm kind of an afterthought to you. Of course a husband always comes first, but I spend a lot of time with my other married friends when their husbands are in town. That's not a criterion for them. This tells me how much they value my friendship, and I appreciate

5 Anonymous, "Rainbow Bridge." Retrieved December 16, 2015, from http://rainbowsbridge.com/Poem.htm.

that." Shut the bitch down. She'll chalk it up to her belief that you're angry because your husband died. Little does she know you don't give a rat's ass whether she forgives you—her self-serving attitude has already crossed her off your list.

2.) A couple days' notice usually suffices for a lunch, and a same-day invite is fine for coffee, a drink, or a cone. If you set a time too far ahead you run the risk of dreading it and canceling due to conflicts you subconsciously summon to rescue you from the looming date.

3.) It doesn't always have to be about food. You gotta keep svelte. And some people eat so slowly that before you know it you've squandered your entire day, trying not to roll your eyes as you watch them chew an enormous salad and attempt to engage you in successive dangling conversations.

4.) Always take your own car. During nighttime hours you may want to chauffeur others if you'll be leaving an event late and don't want to walk to your car alone. It's ultimately your decision when to leave if you're driving the bus. You may need to escape if the event gets too long, boring or dangerous. And if you have wheels you won't have to worry about whether your friends are too drunk to drive (you know you won't be). You need an escape hatch so you can avoid unwanted predators and extricate yourself from over-orchestrated, unending events.

5.) Don't suffocate yourself with confining routines. There's nothing wrong with a weekly tennis date with friends who have proven their loyalty, so long as each participant has the privilege of canceling occasionally, no questions asked. Too much intimacy with casual friends, however, is risky, particularly if they are jealous of you for any reason. You have no time for the stress caused by having the personal details of your life, including your grieving process, being broadcast with a spin to the world at large without your consent or knowledge.

6.) Have one or two friends with whom you can share your innermost thoughts and feelings. At least one of these friends should be someone who herself has endured a spouse's death. Only she will get it. In addition to my family, I am blessed with two such friends. I will always be grateful for their kindness, encouragement, and guidance through the darkness. Only those who have experienced this loss can fully understand the pain and appreciate the occasional glimpses of light and joy which follow it gently over time. Attempting to identify time frames for onset of these starkly contrasting feelings can be frustrating; they come at times of their own choosing.

7.) If you are invited to someone's house, take a gift: a loaf of bread, a bottle of wine, something. You'd be surprised how many people fail to do this, and for no good reason other than laziness and/or selfishness.

8.) Pick friends you can share a laugh with— nonjudgmental friends who can extract humor from stress and chaos. I once overheard an exchange between a bookstore clerk and a customer purchasing *How to Treat Anxiety with Natural Remedies.* "It's easy," the clerk said, "Just fly me to the Montana hills and airdrop food and books once a week." Some people are just quick. No doubt this clerk helped the customer, who left with a smile and probably less

anxiety. Find, enjoy and cultivate friends like this—
they are rarer than moonrock.

And some folks provide comic relief without even knowing it—for instance, "Jimbo," an office colleague who would water your dead plants if you asked him to—Jimbo is very loyal and he will be loyal to you. He has christened himself the firm's "accountant" based upon prior part-time temporary employment as a bank teller. But he has never quite mastered any bookkeeping software. His calculator paper is constantly jamming, requiring numerous phone calls to the manufacturer and a number of special trips to the post office on company time to send it in for repair. He is obsessed with going through channels even if the "chain" of command is only two people deep. His "research" consists of texting more knowledgeable employees and earnestly repeating their wisdom as if it were his own. He can talk for hours in painful detail about cornbread recipes and what covered dish his wife brought to the last church picnic or where they went on their honeymoon. Trivial banter is his game; TMI his M.O. The workplace comic relief he provides far outweighs the annoyance of his interruptions. Dropkicking him into reality is entertaining—he's languished for so long on Planet Jimbo where life is good and everything works out. And he will listen to you. In return for this reality check, Jimbo makes you smile, reinforcing a habit that's essential to your transformation. You love Jimbo on some level, but alas, he is "taken" (mostly with himself).

E. Career

Start a business or get a grant for something near and dear. Find a part-time job in an industry that fascinates you. Maybe there was a calling you had years ago that you never had time to pursue, even something back as far as your teenage years before you met your soul mate or attended your first dance. Nursing, perhaps, or writing or teaching. Whether you aspired to be a puppet, a pirate or a poet, be one now. It's never too late.

"Career" includes valuable volunteer work and hobbies. Help out at your local food pantry. Buy a new computer (the best one you can afford) and take computer lessons. Help someone in your family who needs encouragement. One hundred may be the new forty in light of stem cell developments. You are not over.[6]

---

[6] "I am not over," William Shatner as Denny Crane in *Boston Legal*

XV

Mechanical and Electronic Secrets Men Keep to Themselves

It usually boils down to plugs, wires and batteries. Check these things first. Even a mouse can have a battery, if it's wireless. Men think only they can fix things; they are wrong. When you encounter a technological problem, if you're sitting down, stand up, and if you're standing up, sit down. Then take a deep breath, say "okay" to yourself in a calming manner, and then shift your gears, allowing your rage at the situation to melt away. Say a prayer. Then go get a powerful flashlight and a toolbox and have at it. You can do it. Be patient, logical, and focused.

Here are some really easy fixes:

Plugs. Some sockets don't work. If an electronic device won't turn on, try plugging in a device that you know works—say, for instance, your Elvis Painting that Lights up and Cries—into the suspect socket. Better yet, your bubble head hair dryer from the Sixties.

Folding wooden doors that come off their tracks. This can be maddening. There's a simple trick—punch the wheel down from the top, and it slips right back onto the track. Why didn't they tell us this? Because they want us to think they are geniuses.

Computers. On and off is the panacea. Numerous non-virus issues can be solved merely by turning the computer completely off, and then waiting for a minute before you turn it back on. Some of the newerfangled machines will even walk you through a fix. Which brings me back to my previous advice: Buy the best computer you can afford. Get it professionally installed and connected to your other devices.

This bears repeating: *Buy the best computer you can afford.* Sales folk will happily help enforce this rule. Thank them for it. Forget about delving into the bowels of each machine's specifications. You won't understand them anyway. And annoyance will creep into your last nerve if you ask a question in a big box store to some arrogant, overweight twenty-year-old who looks down his nose at you (assuming you can even get him to look up from his phone). Reading online reviews can sometimes be helpful, though skip pedants whining that some obscure technology need wasn't met. And the braggarts showing off for what they misperceive as a riveted audience.

Replace your peripheral devices when you buy a new computer. Don't try to patch an antique printer into your brand-new laptop. If it works at all, it won't be for long. And take your nephew or your grandson along. These kids know lots about specifications and can interface with the sales person on your behalf.

Once you command a computer to do something, back off and let it follow your instruction even if you realize that's not what you wanted after all. Let it save face. Enough already with the random clicking. Let it prove its loyalty to you, and its love. Multiple signals and demands simply jam up the entrance ramp. If a computer is buzzing or humming or screwing around, if the little circle is twirling or the hourglass filling, let it finish what it started. The machine can really only do one thing *well* at a time, regardless of sales puffing to the contrary. Let it do that thing without interruption from your impatient fingertips.

Paper shredders. Some shredders may claim to be "ten-sheet" shredders. Don't believe it. Only put in seven or eight sheets at once. And let the shredder breathe. Don't keep jamming things in there for fifteen straight minutes. Sending a paper shredder back to the manufacturer is not cost efficient, and the store where you bought it may have a very time-limited return policy. Baby the thing, and it will return the favor a thousandfold. And if it does jam, follow the instructions in the manual. What works with my shredder is turning it off, unplugging it, letting it cool completely down, and then digging out the shreds with eyebrow tweezers. It's actually kind of fun and provides a well-deserved distraction. But if it jams again and you were using it correctly, ditch it. You don't have time to pamper faulty equipment or to deal with medical treatment necessitated by its use.

Printers. If it jams, don't frantically yank out the paper. Look in the online manual for instructions on how to clear paper jams and follow them. If you can't find the manual, Google the name of your printer's make and model number, along with the phrase "paper jam." With the right search words, you can find the answer to about anything—and if you can't, there are many online communities out there[7] where you can post a question and sit back while tech geeks trip over each other to solve your problem first. I have found that YouTube videos are often quite helpful, particularly if you include in your search the particular version of the software about which you have a question.

---

[7] For instance, discussions.apple.com for Apple users

Don't fill the paper tray to the maximum capacity it claims it can handle. You will have significantly fewer paper jams if you follow this simple advice. Same principle for the automatic document feeder. Treat it well, let it rest, and don't ask too much of it even if it could handle the challenge in a crunch. You may need to call upon it when that crunch happens, but don't tax it routinely.

Few office issues cause more stress than toner—being out of it, determining whose fault it is that you are out of it, cleaning it up, and its exorbitant cost. Keep at least one spare toner or ink cartridge on hand, and order at least one new cartridge the day you replace your old one. Same with the drum. However, if your machine is on its last leg, don't get stuck with a bunch of extra accessories that you've bought so far ahead of time you've missed the window for returning them when your machine crashes.

Some online reviews of printers mention that a given model blows a certain type of circuit breaker. Read these reviews carefully, then call an expert electrician and/or a representative from the printer manufacturer before you buy a new printer. Printers are a hassle to return and you don't need the stress of blowing a fuse each time you try to print out a solution for how not to blow a fuse. Being plagued by this sort of techno-paradox will not start your day off well.

Color-coding and pictures. You may think you don't know where to plug cords into the back of a computer, but they're often color-coded. And next to the hole in the computer where you insert a USB cable, is a picture of a USB plug. If you're moving and your wires are not color-coded, tag all of your cords with descriptions of what they plug into, so you're not piecing together a thousand-piece puzzle when you get to your new home. Routers are a hassle to do yourself unless you really have all day and unlimited minutes on your phone.

Installing a wireless device will be the subject of a separate book--*by a different author.*

Flashlights and your own two eyes. Keep a small LED flashlight in every room and in your car. Install a flashlight app on your smartphone. Most things can be figured out if you can see what you are doing—looking for a staple on the floor so your dog won't eat it, looking for a USB port on your computer, figuring out which socket goes with which device, straightening out cords and searching the floor of your car. Also note that flashlights help even during daylight hours where there is some light, particularly when searching for something on a carpet.

It's truly amazing how much you can fix if you start just by looking at it and seeing how it works. I once repaired the internal mechanism of a telephone that I had slammed down too hard. In some ways I did not deserve such an easy fix, but repairing the phone provided a huge sense of accomplishment. Although I would not advise dismantling a computer, you might try it on a small, easily replaceable device that's on its last legs anyway. But give yourself a time limit that you won't exceed no matter how much you love that Kit Kat Clock. Know when to quit.

Reliable computer guy. Be lucky enough, as I am, to have a wonderful nephew who knows everything there is to know about computers. He can do in five minutes what would take other experts hours, or me days and a few crash courses (assuming I could even accomplish the task without voiding the warranty). You may have such a nephew and/or grandchild and not even know it if you've been too wrapped up with your own grief. If after reasonable investigation you find that you have no such nephew, then by all means, hire a computer guy with a reputation for responsiveness. Even if he doesn't know the answer to your question, he will take the initiative to find it. Find someone trustworthy who will tell you when it's no longer cost-effective to continue repairing your old computer. Get help with a new install—you'll save yourself hours of headache. But prepare a list of what you want done, and make sure ahead of time that you know PRECISELY what equipment you need so the guy isn't there twiddling his thumbs at his hourly rate while you run around buying hubs or cables or whatever the whatnot he dreams up.

XVI

Awakening Your Inner Rabbit

Deep within each of us is a sleeping rabbit waiting to be pulled out of a hat. Your rabbit has descended into Stage 3 sleep since you lost your soul mate. Something has worked for you in the past—maybe a magical party dress or a necklace you wore in Acapulco. Maybe that amulet is a long conversation with an old friend from California who although she was nowhere near engaged, bought a wedding dress for $10.00 that was two sizes too small and therefore unzippable. A spark of inspiration can begin with the heartfelt spontaneity reflected in the daily lives of your interesting friends. Find something to set the tone of unique yet comfortable amusement, whether it's a line from a movie[8] or pearly white dogs. Avoid toxic gossip and those eager to spread it. Surround yourself with people who will help and encourage you. A welcoming calm and positivity must prevail to coax the rabbit out of the hat.

The solution comes when you least expect it—maybe even in a fortune cookie: "Learn Chinese." Or maybe

---

[8] "I have come here to chew bubblegum and kick ass . . . and I'm all out of bubblegum," Roddy Piper as John Nada in *They Live* (1988)

a sense that someone from your past is trying to contact you. Solutions to personal problems can emerge just like solutions to computer problems after seemingly random troubleshooting and thinking outside the box. Nothing is truly random. You know when that solution comes, that God had a hand in it; only through Him could the solution have come through so clearly through the chaos. You have a sense that you are part of something bigger. And when the rabbit-in-waiting emerges from the hat, you will know what you need to do.

XVII

Be Ready and in the Moment!

We are often asked to bear devastating loss at a time in life when we are least able to withstand it. When we are sixty and lose a spouse, the pain and fear are not tempered by youth's optimism. The fear of being alone is greater now than at twenty. Fear of having nowhere to go on Christmas Day other than a ladies' brunch where you will munch politely on sliced turkey sandwiches served on paper plates atop worn TV trays.

But don't marry or move in with someone due to fear of loneliness. Some married people are more alone than many singles. There are much worse things than being alone. Solitude requires planning, some scheduling of events with others, and frequent initiative.

Exude confidence and remain at the ready for positive personal and professional encounters. Be proud of yourself. Don't go to the grocery store looking bummy. Don't go out in scratched shoes or carry grimy purses. Get a light shade of lipstick. Wear hip jewelry. Stand up straight. And smile. Use those white strips on your teeth. And don't constantly fold into your phone in public. Make eye contact. With real people.

Be ready. Throw out the dull, drab clothing that makes you look boxy, tired, and old. Keep caught up with your laundry so you can wear that favorite shirt or pair of jeans and don't have to fish for it in the laundry or wear it for more days than appropriate in polite society. Try things on that you have never worn together. This fosters creativity and makes you feel new. Avoid fuddy duddy sections of department stores, such as those which house clothing with excessive floral patterns. Opt for cut-rate shops with fashionable clothing instead. Geometric patterns that don't hurt your eyes are a good place to start. Soft colors can balance geometrical harshness; this combination will keep you poised and in control.

Stay caught up on your work. Otherwise, the burden of being behind will grasp you in its unyielding talons when you should be out making things happen. Assume responsibility for being ready to receive your God-given destiny.

Don't be discouraged if someone says no. Each rejection shows you a new, more refined and inviting path. And when the person who rejected you calls back after his schedule clears, you're busy. Keep all of your friendships solid, and don't insist on having everyone attend each and every minor gathering. A particular friend may have planned something with you because he or she has a problem to discuss privately. A third person can misalign the planets.

When you walk your dog, let him lead sometimes. Slow down. Let him stop and listen, stalk some prey. This is his outing, and an important journey for you both. If he enjoys it, you will too. He can flush out squirrels and rabbits. This will make him feel powerful. Give him that joy. He's done his job if this potential prey scrambles up a trunk, and he will march proudly on. This interaction connects you with life again.

Shower and apply makeup before you go out. Keep your car washed and your mind alert. Dress with color even if you occasionally garner an unwanted reptilian glare. Look nice for you. The power red platform shoes or form-fitting jeans will put you where you deserve to be.

The Five Circles of Life may occasionally or frequently be in chaos now, but if you follow the simple principles outlined in this book, they won't be for long. Allow yourself time for friends, and time to rejoice in the short moments of calm reflection you carve out of each day. These moments fill the hole in your heart you may have thought could never be repaired. Put your shoulders back, stand up straight, and literally pat yourself on the back. No pain could rival the pain you experienced when you came home to an empty house after the funeral or the final divorce hearing. But the worst is behind you. Expect occasional waves of sadness and discontent, but take joy in the moments of contentment, as you sit with your dog curled up in your lap and watch yet another episode of the latest bridal series. Be glad that you now hold the remote and no longer have to worry about the channel being changed just as the plot crescendos. Although electric shadows will not pay your bills or take you to dinner, they can get you through a rough patch, and holding that remote with your favorite four-legger nearby is quite empowering. But set a time limit on your TV watching, and no matter how hard it is, get back to enjoying life and the exciting things that lie in store for you. Now is your time to push beyond just getting by and get back to being happy.

As you restore order from the chaos, respect the grieving process. Its plot works best when allowed to unfold in its own time, interspersed with beauty and stillness.

Spiritual, physical, family, friend, and career spheres will guide you when you are ready— "When the pupil is ready the teacher will appear."[9] A mentor or colleague may identify your strengths and weaknesses, or your inner rabbit may unfold the magic as your personal spheres sync briefly with each other. Now may be your final opportunity to listen to what is calling you. Take your chance.[10]

---

[9] Plato

[10] YouTube can be inspiring, mentally challenging and fun. Positive religious messages of encouragement and hope—Joel Osteen's messages, for instance, which often cross denominational lines—motivate many listeners to remain positive. YouTube provides an opportunity to select from a vast variety of brief, insightful messages. You might try Eckhart Tolle, Gregg Braden, and other visionaries and spiritual leaders to whom YouTube or your heart may guide you.

Listen to upbeat songs that you have always loved. Try watching Mick Jagger dancing in a purple tank top to "Start Me Up"—you will understand the meaning of "Moves Like Jagger" by Maroon Five. Meghan Trainor's "Dear Future Husband" infuses confidence and provides upbeat back tempo while you're googling for a plumber. And when you're ready to work out, try John Fogerty's "Centerfield" or Taylor Swift's "Shake It Off." When all else fails, watch *I Love Lucy*—the fact that we are closer now in age to Fred and Ethel than we were when we first watched only enhances our capacity for empathy and humor.

Epilogue

"Don't cry because it's over. Smile because it happened."[11] Remember that even death cannot tear from you the many happy memories of your relationship. Treasure them and in doing so you will honor your soul mate's memory and your own worth as well—you're the one he loved, after all. You have been loved, and for that you are lucky. Many search their entire lives for love and don't find it. It's okay to cry sometimes, but your sadness will be short-lived and followed by peaceful contentment if you gradually allow good times to take center stage.

---

[11] Often attributed to Dr. Seuss, sometimes to Gabriel García Márquez